SHAKESPEARE'S LOVERS

A Text for Performance and Analysis

Libby Appel and Michael Flachmann

SOUTHERN ILLINOIS UNIVERSITY PRESS
Carbondale and Edwardsville

Copyright ©1983 by the
Board of Trustees, Southern Illinois University
ALL RIGHTS RESERVED
Printed in the United States of America
Edited by Teresa White
Designed by Design for Publishing, Bob Nance
Production supervised by John DeBacher

Library of Congress Cataloging in Publication Data

Shakespeare, William, 1564-1616.
  Shakespeare's lovers.

  Bibliography: p.
  1. Love—Drama. I. Appel, Libby, 1937-
II. Flachmann, Michael. III. Title.
PR2774.A2   1983   822.3'3   82-5444
ISBN 0-8093-1072-4   AACR2

To Mark Lamos

Contents

Preface

This project first took shape when we began working together at the California Shakespearean Festival in Visalia. Our original concept was to bring together a collection of scenes, songs, and sonnets and to arrange them as a script for production that illustrated the theme of love in Shakespeare. Taken out of their former contexts, the scenes were to make up a fresh, new context; themes and ideas from many plays were to be fused into an "original" play that explored Shakespeare's universal, enduring, fully human views about love in a variety of settings—many single threads, so to speak, woven into a rich Shakespearean tapestry of romance. Following a successful staging of this play by the Festival's Journeymen, a group of sixteen young actors and actresses with minor roles in the Visalia professional company, we decided to publish *Shakespeare's Lovers* so that it could reach an even wider audience.

Shakespeare's Lovers exists principally as a play to be rehearsed and acted on stage. Four dramatic sections chronicle the pursuit of romantic fulfillment: "Discovering Love," "Seeking Advice about Love," "Having Problems with Love," and "Finding Solutions to Love's Problems." The progression from one section to the next, from one scene to another, is accomplished by a Narrator who promises to "conjure" the audience with the magic of Shakespeare's words and images. Every single word in this text, in fact, comes directly from Shakespeare.

Shakespeare's Lovers can also be used by theater students to isolate certain Shakespearean scenes for in-class acting experience. Those involved in classroom scene study can concentrate on character relationships and motivation, textual problems, and other complexities of the acting process (such as voice, diction, and stage movement) without the immediate concern of placing the scene into the larger, more intricate context of an entire Shakespearean drama. Nor will these student actors have to carry with them a copy of *The Complete Works of Shakespeare* to have immediate access to a great number of scenes from the dramatist's most popular plays. This small, single text is the only ingredient necessary for hundreds of profitable hours of scene study in the classroom.

This script will also prove useful to English teachers who wish to introduce their students of dramatic literature to a variety of Shakespearean love themes and characters in a relatively brief amount of time. After reading *Shakespeare's Lovers*, many students will want to learn more about the scenes and situations they encountered in the classroom; this text,therefore, is a means of stimulating students to explore further the fascinating world of Shakespearean drama.

We believe that the plays of Shakespeare are best understood if they are approached as "scripts for action." In other words, we see a relationship between the printed play and its performance on stage that is clearly similar to the dependency between a piece of sheet music and its orchestral performance or between a recipe in a cookbook and the *coq au vin* which results. The script of a play is a pattern for performance, a recipe for a particular blend of sound, motion, and stage magic. To ignore this crucial interdependence and to treat plays solely as novels ripe for analysis is to neglect the dominant purpose of this particular art form. Shakespeare's works were meant to be staged; the meaning of each play, each scene, each line, will therefore exist most fully in production. For this reason, we believe that students from theater and English should be encouraged to act out scenes from *Shakespeare's Lovers* as often as possible—either in the classroom or on the stage. Only by playing the parts will they find truly meaningful pathways into the plays.

The textual apparatus that accompanies *Shakespeare's Lovers* supports our contention that Shakespeare's plays are "scripts" intended to be staged. To the right of each page of text is a clear, understandable glossary that defines difficult words; at the foot of these pages are occasional longer notes that comment on obscure or obtuse references; and on each facing left-hand page are suggested stage directions. We have deliberately created a theatrical prompt-book format by the oversized pages and by the amount of blank space available in the left-hand pages on which notes, ideas, and more elaborate stage directions may be recorded. As most students have found, writing notes in the margins of the text will be easier and more useful than the standard practice of using a separate notebook.

The following Introduction offers production advice that will be helpful principally to directors wishing to stage a full-scale performance of *Shakespeare's Lovers*. The suggestions were largely drawn from ideas developed during the script's first production in Visalia. More experienced directors may decide to ignore many of these recommendations in favor of their own ideas, while others will find the advice entirely useful. Completing the extratextual apparatus are a Commentary, which discusses each scene in the script and its function within its original play, and sheet music for each of the four songs in *Shakespeare's Lovers*: "When Griping Griefs the Heart Doth Wound," "Take, O Take Those Lips Away," "It Was a Lover and His Lass," and "Who Is Silvia?" Also included is a catalogue of all the Shakespearean scenes used in the script and a brief list of suggested sources for further reading on Renaissance life, society, and the theme of love in Shakespeare's plays.

We gratefully acknowledge the support and assistance of the following people: for scholarly insight, Murph Swander; for photographs, Micha Langer; for reviews of the manuscript, Sam Smiley, Carol Raff, Paul Appel, Patti Reed, Mary Chandler, and Kim Flachmann; for typing the final draft, Jilanie Wheeler; and, finally, for energy and inspiration, David Fox-Brenton, Alan Levey, and the 1980 California Shakespearean Festival Journeymen.

L. A.
M. C. F.

Introduction

The Ensemble

Eleven members make up the ensemble—six men and five women. If a particular group of players has more actors to add to the company, each actor will then reduce the number of roles he or she plays. One man is the storyteller, the Narrator, and he remains the direct link between the actors and the audience throughout the play. The plot should seem to spring from the Narrator's thoughts as he manipulates the action. The Narrator will play several roles, changing in and out of them with the rest of the ensemble as he tells the story. The other ten actors also play numerous characters, and the audience is always aware that the same group of actors fills many roles.

No attempt should be made to costume each scene elaborately or accurately. The actors should remain in a basic outfit—contemporary rehearsal clothes, for example—and occasionally add pieces to help distinguish new characters in new situations. Continuity would be maintained, moreover, if recurring characters, such as Beatrice and Benedick, are played by the same actors. The emphasis at all times should be on the flow of action. Scenes do not need to be announced; a program note listing the scenes is sufficient (or a scenic device could be employed to display the title of the play as the scene is in progress).

The Music and the Musician

The music for the textual songs may be entirely drawn from sources of English Renaissance music (see "Music" section), or it may be newly composed to suit the style of the individual production. If the musician is particularly sensitive to the script, the ensemble, and the narrative action, he or she could improvise all of the musical bridges and underscore the action of many of the scenes during the performance. Even if the music is wholly original, an Elizabethan flavor should be retained. At least one musician is required as an additional member of the ensemble. The Narrator and other members of the company might also play instruments. Since the music is an important and highly effective element in the script, the musician should remain in full view of the audience at all times.

The Playing Area

The entire ensemble (including the musician) remains onstage throughout the play. All scenes are generated out of the group assemblage. Most of the scenes take place in a central space, the playing area, which is distinct from an ensemble area where the actors are gathered. When their scene is about to be presented, actors will move from the ensemble area to the playing area; at the conclusion of the scene, the actors will return to their former places with the rest of the ensemble. Members of the ensemble should feel free to react emotionally to the action taking place before them and to the words and gestures of the Narrator during the bridges between scenes.

The ensemble should change positions for the four separate movements of the play: "Discovering Love," "Seeking Advice about Love," "Having Problems with Love," and "Finding Solutions to Love's Problems." This physical shift will help the audience understand the changes which occur within the overall flow of the action.

Platforms or a large central stairway or stair units may be used to seat the actors in the ensemble area. Although the ensemble's presence is always felt on stage, lighting can help to isolate areas and determine focus. Minimal props should be used. All props and costume pieces should be onstage with the actors and the musician. The principal effect is that all the action of the play springs out of one central group identity.

The Promptbook

This text has been designed as a director's and actor's promptbook. The glossary definitions run parallel to the text on the right to help explain difficult words and phrases. The suggested stage directions on the left-hand side of the text serve as a skeletal outline for movement and action. Directors and actors should write additional stage blocking and character motivations on this facing left-hand page as such actions are discovered and explored in rehearsals.

The Text

The entire text of *Shakespeare's Lovers* has been newly edited from the most authoritative manuscripts extant. The 1623 First Folio served as the copy text for most selections, though scenes taken from the following plays are indebted to earlier sources: *Romeo and Juliet* (the Second Quarto of 1599), *Much Ado about Nothing* (the 1600 Quarto), *The Merchant of Venice* (the First Quarto of 1600), *Henry IV, Part I* (the 1598 First Quarto), *Pericles* (the 1609 First quarto), and *The Passionate Pilgrim* (the 1599 Octavo). Throughout, spelling and punctuation have been modernized and standardized. In footnoting obscure words and phrases, the authors have relied upon *The Oxford English Dictionary* and other general reference works. Specific scenes have been identified within brackets in the text, though no attempt has been made to mention which words, phrases, and lines have been omitted within those scenes.

ACT I

Beginning in the darkness, coming from the ensemble area, continuing as the lights fade up.

Narrator steps forward out of the ensemble area into the playing area.

PART I
Discovering Love

VOICES
Love
Pure love
First best love [*Music.*]
My heart's dear love
Heavenly love   5
Best love
Firm love
Good love
Great love
Sole possessor of my love [*Music.*]   10
First best love
Innocent love
Faithful love
Sweet heart
Dearest chuck   15
Everlasting love
Kind love
First best love
Perfect love
Love-sick love   20
Most best, most dearest
ALL VOICES
First best love [*Music.*]
NARRATOR
O for a muse of fire, that would ascend
The brightest heaven of invention.
A kingdom for a stage, princes to act,   25
And monarchs to behold the swelling scene.
VOICES
Firm love
Equal love
Sweet chuck
Ever-preserved love   30
Great love

Narrator moves closer to the audience.

Three men and three women move to their dancing positions as the music changes to a Renaissance Allemand or Galliard. The other two women join the Musician and play recorders or lutes. As the music begins, the three men and women dance. Two unattached men stand to the side and watch the couples. The Narrator joins the two men.

The two men and the Narrator who have been watching move toward the dancing couples and cut in; the men who were dancing join the unattached women and the Musician. Romeo and Juliet cross to center stage as the dancing continues around them; soon, they are surrounded in silhouetted shadow by the other two couples.

The couples are dancing to an Elizabethan Galliard or Allemand. Romeo and Juliet's rhythm is slightly slower than that of the two other couples.

ALL VOICES
First best love [*Music.*]
NARRATOR
I am a magician. My way is to conjure you, and I'll begin with
the women. I charge you, O women, for the love you bear to
men, to like as much of this play as please you. And I charge   35
you, O men, for the love you bear to women — as I perceive by
your simpering none of you hates them — that between you and
the women, the play may please.
VOICES
Pure love   40
Innocent love
ALL VOICES
First best love [*Music.*]

[*Romeo and Juliet,* I.v]

FIRST MALE
O, she doth teach the torches to burn bright!
SECOND MALE
It seems she hangs upon the cheek of night.
FIRST MALE
Like a rich jewel in an Ethiope's ear.
SECOND MALE
Beauty too rich for use, for earth too dear!
ROMEO
The measure done, I'll watch her place of stand,
And, touching hers, make blessed my rude hand.
ROMEO
If I profane with my unworthiest hand
This holy shrine, the gentle sin is this:
My lips, two blushing pilgrims, ready stand
To smooth that rough touch with a tender kiss.
JULIET
Good pilgrim, you do wrong your hand too much,
Which mannerly devotion shows in this:
For saints have hands that pilgrims' hands do touch,
And palm to palm is holy palmers' kiss.
ROMEO
Have not saints lips, and holy palmers too?   15

Like...ear: like an earring worn by an exotic Ethiopian.
dear: expensive, valuable.
5
rude: rough, uncivilized.

This holy shrine: Juliet's hand, which Romeo is holding.

mannerly: proper.

7–20 These lines, in the form of an English sonnet, are followed by a quatrain.

14 holy palmer: a pilgrim whose journey to the holy land was symbolized by a palm leaf (the entire dialogue puns on the meaning of Romeo's name: one who takes a pilgrimage).

Romeo stops dancing.

Juliet attempts to return to the dance.

Romeo holds Juliet and prevents her from dancing.

He kisses her.

Romeo kisses her a second time.
The dancers stop, applaud the musicians, and return to the ensemble area as the music concludes. Miranda and Ferdinand emerge from the group of returning dancers to prepare their
scene. The Narrator steps to the edge of the playing area to observe the action. Ferdinand looks
fondly at Miranda.

Ferdinand exits to the ensemble area to bring in a large log.

Miranda moves to a place where she can watch Ferdinand and be unobserved herself.

Ferdinand is dragging logs across the stage; Miranda comes forward to join him.
Miranda indicates a place where Ferdinand may sit near her.

Miranda rises. She pulls at the log in Ferdinand's hand.

Ferdinand tugs the log away from her.

JULIET
Ay, pilgrim, lips that they must use in prayer.
ROMEO
O then, dear saint, let lips do what hands do:
They pray. Grant thou, lest faith turn to despair.

do what hands do: press
together (as in a kiss).
Grant thou: Grant my
request to kiss you.

JULIET
Saints do not move, though grant for prayers' sake.
ROMEO
Then move not while my prayer's effect I take.
Thus from my lips, by thine, my sin is purged.

move not: stand
still.

JULIET
Then have my lips the sin that they have took.
ROMEO
Sin from my lips? O trespass sweetly urged!
Give me my sin again.

again: back again.

JULIET
                            You kiss by the book.

by the book: according
to the rules of
etiquette.

FERDINAND
The very instant that I saw you, did
My heart fly to your service.
NARRATOR
Poor worm, thou art infected!
[*to audience*]   Fair encounter
Of two most rare affections! Heavens rain grace   30
On that which breeds between them!

[*The Tempest*, III.i]

MIRANDA
                            Alas, now, pray you,
Work not so hard. I would the lightning had
Burned up those logs that you are enjoined to pile!
Pray, set it down and rest you. When this burns,
'Twill weep for having wearied you.   5
FERDINAND
                            O most dear mistress,
The sun will set before I shall discharge
What I must strive to do.
MIRANDA
                            If you'll sit down,
I'll bear your logs the while. Pray give me that.   10
I'll carry it to the pile.
FERDINAND
                  No, precious creature,

19 Saints do not move: according to pre-Reformation doctrine, Saints did not intercede between God and mankind unless they were requested to do so through prayer.

She once again attempts to grab the log.

He stops her firmly.

Ferdinand puts down the log and they both sit on it. He looks at her fondly.

Miranda moves away in embarrassment.

Ferdinand crosses to stop her from leaving.

I had rather crack my sinews, break my back,
Than you should such dishonor undergo
While I sit lazy by.   15
MIRANDA
                    It would become me
As well as it does you; and I should do it
With much more ease, for my good will is to it,
And yours it is against. You look wearily.
FERDINAND
No, noble mistress! 'Tis fresh morning with me   20
When you are by at night. I do beseech you—
Chiefly that I might set it in my prayers—
What is your name?
MIRANDA
                    Miranda.
FERDINAND
                              Admired Miranda!   25
Indeed the top of admiration: worth
What's dearest to the world! Full many a lady

best regard: most complete
approval.

I have eyed with best regard, and many a time
The harmony of their tongues hath into bondage

several: different.

Brought my too diligent ear. For several virtues
Have I liked several women—never any

With so full soul: so
unreservedly. owed: owned.

With so full soul but some defect in her
Did quarrel with the noblest grace she owed
And put it to the foil. But you, O you,
So perfect and so peerless, are created   35
Of every creature's best!
MIRANDA
                    I do not know
One of my sex; no woman's face remember,
Save, from my glass, mine own. Nor have I seen
More that I may call men than you, good friend,   40
And my dear father. How features are abroad,

abroad: elsewhere in the
world.

I am skilless of; but, by my modesty,
The jewel in my dower, I would not wish
Any companion in the world but you,
Nor can imagination form a shape,   45
Besides yourself, to like of. But I prattle
Something too wildly.
FERDINAND
                    I am, in my condition,

condition: rank.

26 admiration: wonder or amazement (the name "Miranda" means "wonderful woman").
34 foil: a defeat, as in a "fall" in wrestling (perhaps with a pun on "foil," setting off the contrast between defects and virtues).

Miranda moves closer to Ferdinand.

A prince, Miranda; I do think, a king
(I would, not so!); and would no more endure
This wooden slavery than to suffer
The flesh-fly blow my mouth. Hear my soul speak:
The very instant that I saw you, did
My heart fly to your service; there resides,
To make me slave to it; and for your sake
Am I this patient log-man.

MIRANDA
              Do you love me?

FERDINAND
O heaven, O earth, bear witness to this sound,
And crown what I profess with kind event
If I speak true! If hollowly, invert
What best is boded me to mischief! I,
Beyond all limit of what else in the world,
Do love, prize, honor you.

MIRANDA
            I am a fool
To weep at what I am glad of.

FERDINAND
              Wherefore weep you?

MIRANDA
At mine unworthiness, that dare not offer
What I desire to give, and much less take
What I shall die to want. But this is trifling;
And all the more it seeks to hide itself,
The bigger bulk it shows. Hence, bashful cunning,
And prompt me, plain and holy innocence!
I am your wife, if you will marry me;
If not, I'll die your maid. To be your fellow
You may deny me, but I'll be your servant,
Whether you will or no.

FERDINAND
            My mistress, dearest,
And I thus humble ever.

MIRANDA
              My husband, then?

FERDINAND
Ay, with a heart as willing
As bondage e'er of freedom. Here's my hand.

MIRANDA
And mine, with my heart in it. And now farewell
Till half an hour hence.

Glosses:

50

wooden slavery: being forced to carry wood. *blow my mouth:* defile my mouth by laying eggs in it.

55

with kind event: favorable outcome. *hollowly:* falsely. *boded me:* intended for me (i.e., change the good fortune which is due me to misfortune).

65

want: be without.
70
bashful cunning: coyness. *prompt...innocence:* I would rather be guided by innocence than craft. *fellow:* equal.

80

As Miranda and Ferdinand move toward each other to say farewell, Lucentio, Bianca, and Hortensio come between them, preventing their final embrace. Hortensio carries his lute, Lucentio his books, and Bianca a slate and chalk.

Lucentio and Hortensio surround Bianca.

The men argue in back of, in front of, and over the head of Bianca.

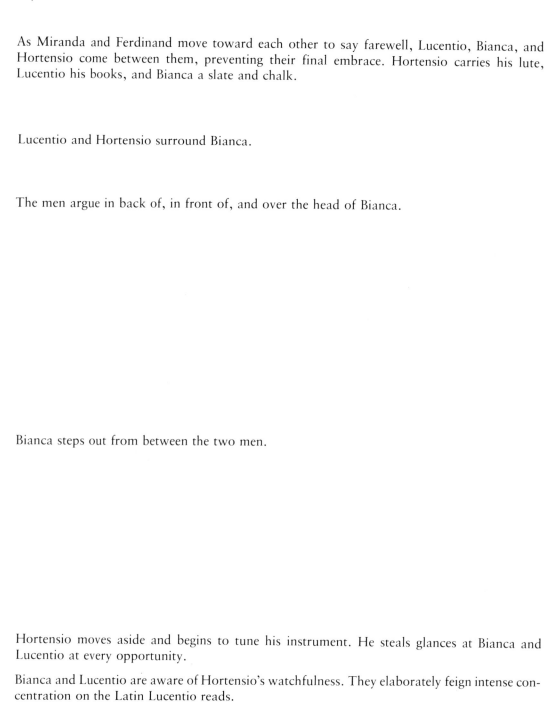

Bianca steps out from between the two men.

Hortensio moves aside and begins to tune his instrument. He steals glances at Bianca and Lucentio at every opportunity.

Bianca and Lucentio are aware of Hortensio's watchfulness. They elaborately feign intense concentration on the Latin Lucentio reads.

FERDINAND

A thousand thousand!

A thousand thousand:
i.e., a thousand farewells.

[*The Taming of the Shrew,* III.i]

LUCENTIO
Fiddler, forbear! You grow too forward, sir.
Have you so soon forgot the entertainment
Her sister Katherine welcomed you withal?
HORTENSIO
But, wrangling pedant, this is
The patroness of heavenly harmony.   5
Then give me leave to have prerogative;   *prerogative:* precedence.
And when in music we have spent an hour,
Your lecture shall have leisure for as much.   *lecture:* lesson.
LUCENTIO
Preposterous ass, that never read so far   *preposterous:* in the sense of
To know the cause why music was ordained!   inverting the natural
Was it not to refresh the mind of man   order of things.
After his studies or his usual pain?   *pain:* labor.
Then give me leave to read philosophy,   *read:* teach.
And, while I pause, serve in your harmony.   *serve in your harmony:*
HORTENSIO   i.e., refresh me by playing
Sirrah, I will not bear these braves of thine.   your instrument. *braves:*
BIANCA   insults.
Why, gentlemen, you do me double wrong
To strive for that which resteth in my choice.
I am no breeching scholar in the schools;   *breeching scholar:* a school-
I'll not be tied to hours nor 'pointed times,   girl deserving a whipping.
But learn my lessons as I please myself.   *'pointed:* appointed.
And, to cut off all strife, here sit we down.
Take you your instrument, play you the whiles;   *the whiles:* meanwhile.
His lecture will be done ere you have tuned.
HORTENSIO
You'll leave his lecture when I am in tune?
LUCENTIO
That will be never. Tune your instrument.   25
BIANCA
Where left we last?
LUCENTIO
Here, madam.

---

5 The patroness of heavenly harmony: Hortensio compares Bianca to Minerva, the goddess of music and the inventor
of musical instruments.

Lucentio dares to whisper his real thoughts to Bianca in between the Latin phrases.

Hortensio suspects the conversation is getting intimate. He moves closer to the couple.

Hortensio plays when Bianca asks him.

Lucentio moves Bianca further away from Hortensio.

Hortensio starts to join them again.

Lucentio stops Hortensio quickly with his words.

Hortensio speaks to the audience in an aside.

When Bianca calls, Hortensio scrambles to join her.

Hortensio motions Lucentio out of the area.

Lucentio starts to leave but stops to watch the couple in order to prevent any advances by Hortensio toward Bianca.

"Hic ibat Simois; hic est Sigeia tellus;
Hic steterat Priami regia celsa senis."

BIANCA
Conster them. 30

LUCENTIO
"Hic ibat," as I told you before, "Simois," I am Lucentio, "hic
est," son unto Vincentio of Pisa, "Sigeia tellus," disguised thus to
get your love; "Hic steterat," and that Lucentio who comes
awooing, "Priami," is my man Tranio, "regia," bearing my port,
"celsa senis," that we might beguile the old pantaloon.

bearing my port: acting as I would. *pantaloon:* foolish old man (a stock character of the *commedia dell'arte*).

HORTENSIO
Madam, my instrument's in tune.

BIANCA
Let's hear. O fie! The treble jars.

jars: makes a discordant sound.

LUCENTIO
Spit in the hole, man, and tune again.

spit in the hole: moisten the hole to make the peg stick.

BIANCA
Now let me see if I can conster it: "Hic ibat Simois," I know you
not, "hic est Sigeia tellus," I trust you not; "Hic steterat Priami," take
heed he hear us not, "regia," presume not, "celsa senis," despair not. 40

HORTENSIO
Madam, 'tis now in tune.

LUCENTIO
All but the base.

HORTENSIO
The base is right. 'Tis the base knave that jars.
How fiery and forward our pedant is!
Now, for my life, the knave doth court my love. 45
Pedascule, I'll watch you better yet.

Pedascule: the Latin vocative of *pedasculus,* "little pedant."

BIANCA
In time I may believe, yet I mistrust.

LUCENTIO
Mistrust it not.

BIANCA
I must believe my master; else, I promise you, 50
I should be arguing still upon that doubt.

doubt: difficult question.

But let it rest. Now, Litio, to you:
Good master, take it not unkindly, pray,
That I have been thus pleasant with you both.

HORTENSIO
You may go walk and give me leave a while. 55
My lessons make no music in three parts.

in three parts: for three voices.

LUCENTIO
Are you so formal, sir? Well, I must wait,

formal: precise.

28–29 "Here flowed the river Simois; here is the Sigeian land; here stood the lofty palace of old Priam" (a letter from Penelope to Ulysses; Ovid's *Epistolae Heroidum,* I).

Hortensio proudly hands Bianca a paper.
Bianca reads.

Bianca turns to Lucentio and smiles at him. She turns back to Hortensio, tears the paper, and throws it away.

Bianca walks back to the ensemble area with Lucentio following closely behind. Hortensio is left, disgruntled, to pick up the lute, books, slate, and the torn sheet of paper.

The Narrator looks at Hortensio and then turns to the audience.

The Narrator assumes the role of Pandarus, crosses to Troilus and Cressida, and brings them forward. Cressida tries to run away; unsuccessful, she hides her face in her shawl.

Pandarus removes the shawl from Cressida's face.
He pushes the two lovers close together.

Troilus and Cressida break apart in embarrassment.

And watch withal; for, but I be deceived,
Our fine musician groweth amorous.

withal: at the same time.
but: unless.

HORTENSIO

Madam, before you touch the instrument,
To learn the order of my fingering,   60
I must begin with rudiments of art,
To teach you gamut in a briefer sort—   *gamut:* scale.
More pleasant, pithy, and effectual
Than hath been taught by any of my trade.
And there it is in writing, fairly drawn.   65

BIANCA

"'Gamut' I am, the ground of all accord,   *ground:* lowest note.
'A re,' to plead Hortensio's passion;   *accord:* harmony.
'B mi,' Bianca, take him for thy lord,
'C fa ut,' that loves with all affection;
'D sol re,' one cleft, two notes have I,   70
'E la mi,' show pity or I die."
Call you this gamut? Tut, I like it not.
Old fashions please me best. I am not so nice   *nice:* capricious.
To change true rules for odd inventions.

NARRATOR

Mistress, your father prays you leave your books   75
And help to dress your sister's chamber up.

BIANCA

Farewell, sweet masters both. I must be gone.

NARRATOR

He is far gone, far gone; and truly in my youth
I suffered much extremity for love, very near this.
Once more I'll mark how love can vary wit.   80
Bring us to this sight, and you shall say
I'll prove a busy actor in their play.

[*Troilus and Cressida*, III.ii]

NARRATOR

Come, come, what need you blush? Shame's a baby. Here she is
now. Swear the oaths now to her that you have sworn to me.
What, are you gone again? You must be watched ere you be   *watched:* kept awake
made tame, must you? Come your ways, come your ways. Why   (one method of training a
do you not speak to her? Come, draw this curtain, and let's see   hawk). *curtain:* veil.
your picture. Alas the day, how loath you are to offend daylight!
An 'twere dark, you'd close sooner. So, so; rub on, and kiss the   *close:* come together or
mistress. How now! Nay, you shall fight your hearts out ere I part you.   come to terms (as in a legal

---

70 C fa ut: in the gamut of Hortensio, which begins on G instead of C, this note is the fourth (*fa*) in a scale of G, but
the first (*ut* or *do*) in a major scale based on C.

Pandarus attempts to bring the two to a more private place.

The Narrator (Pandarus) walks away and observes the action. Cressida follows behind Pandarus attempting, shyly, to show Troilus the way inside.

Troilus holds his ground.

Pandarus returns.

Cressida turns sharply on Pandarus.

Leering at the two, Pandarus steps out of their view but stays close to the playing area.

Cressida crosses closer to Troilus.

TROILUS
You have bereft me of all words, lady.

PANDARUS
Words pay no debts; give her deeds. Come in, come in.

CRESSIDA
Will you walk in, my lord?

TROILUS
O Cressid, how often have I wished me thus!

CRESSIDA
Wished, my lord? The gods grant—O my lord!

TROILUS
What should they grant? What makes this pretty
abruption? What curious dreg espies my sweet lady
in the fountain of our love?

CRESSIDA
More dregs than water, if my fears have eyes.

TROILUS
O, let my lady apprehend no fear. In all Cupid's pageant there is
presented no monster.

CRESSIDA
Nor nothing monstrous neither?   20

PANDARUS
What, blushing still? Have you not done talking yet?

CRESSIDA
Well, uncle, what folly I commit, I dedicate to you.

PANDARUS
I thank you for that. If my lord get a boy of you, you'll give him
me. Be true to my lord. If he flinch, chide me for it.

TROILUS
You know now your hostages—your uncle's word and my firm faith.   25

CRESSIDA
Boldness comes to me now and brings me heart.
Prince Troilus, I have loved you night and day
For many weary months.

TROILUS
Why was my Cressid then so hard to win?

CRESSIDA
Hard to seem won. But I was won, my lord,   30
With the first glance that ever—pardon me;
If I confess much, you will play the tyrant.
I love you now, but not, till now, so much
But I might master it. In faith, I lie.
My thoughts were like unbridled children, grown   35
Too headstrong for their mother. See, we fools!
Why have I blabbed? Who shall be true to us
When we are so unsecret to ourselves?

agreement). *An 'twere*: if it
were. *rub...mistress*:
Pandarus puns on terms
from lawn bowling.

abruption: breaking off.
curious: causing care or
concern. *dreg*: sediment,
residue.

Cressida moves very close to Troilus and puts his hand on her mouth.

Cressida seems ready for a kiss.
Troilus overcomes his shyness and fears and kisses her.

Pandarus calls to them from the side.

Cressida hears Pandarus and draws away from Troilus. She starts to exit.

Troilus crosses to stop her. He holds her still.

But, though I loved you well, I wooed you not.
And yet, good faith, I wished myself a man—   40
Or that we women had men's privilege
Of speaking first. Sweet, bid me hold my tongue,
For in this rapture I shall surely speak
The thing I shall repent. See, see, your silence,
Cunning in dumbness, from my weakness draws   45
My very soul of counsel! Stop my mouth.

soul of counsel: my most secret thoughts. *Stop my mouth:* i.e., with a kiss. *albeit:* although.

TROILUS
And shall, albeit sweet music issues thence.
PANDARUS
Pretty, in faith!
CRESSIDA
My lord, I do beseech you, pardon me;
'Twas not my purpose thus to beg a kiss.   50
I am ashamed. O heavens, what have I done?
For this time will I take my leave, my lord.
TROILUS
Your leave, sweet Cressid?
CRESSIDA
Pray you, content you.
TROILUS
What offends you, lady?   55
CRESSIDA
Sir, mine own company.
TROILUS
You cannot shun yourself.
CRESSIDA
Let me go and try.
TROILUS
                    O Cressid,
I am as true as truth's simplicity,   60
And simpler than the infancy of truth.
Yet, after all comparisons of truth,
As truth's authentic author to be cited,
"As true as Troilus" shall crown up the verse
And sanctify the numbers.   *numbers:* verses.
CRESSIDA
                    Prophet may you be!
If I be false, or swerve a hair from truth,
When time is old and hath forgot itself,
When waterdrops have worn the stones of Troy,
And blind oblivion swallowed cities up,   70
And mighty states characterless are grated   *characterless:* without leaving a mark.
To dusty nothing, yet let memory,
From false to false, among false maids in love,

Pandarus crosses between them and takes their hands.

Troilus and Cressida are gazing in each other's eyes as Pandarus holds their hands firmly clasped together.

Pandarus tries to pull the lovers out of the playing area.

The Narrator, as Pandarus, leads Troilus and Cressida back to their places in the ensemble area. The man walks over to the narrator, gesturing toward Troilus.

Richard and Anne come forward. Another man, playing the dead Henry, lies on stage. The Narrator, still keeping a little of Pandarus's "mantle" on himself, watches Richard as Richard watches Anne. It is unnecessary to portray Richard's physical deformities in this scene. Taken out of context of the play, the scene explores passionate dualities of hate and sexual passion.

Anne kneels beside the body.

Anne rises and gestures to the Narrator to move the body.

Upbraid my falsehood! When they have said "as false
As air, as water, wind, or sandy earth,   75
As fox to lamb, or wolf to heifer's calf,
Pard to the hind, or stepdame to her son,"   *Pard*: Leopard.
Yea, let me say, to stick the heart of falsehood,
"As false as Cressid."

PANDARUS

Go to, a bargain made. Seal it! Seal it! I'll be the witness. Here I   80
hold your hand, here my cousin's. If ever you prove false one to
another, since I have taken such pains to bring you together, let all
pitiful goers-between be called to the world's end after my name: Call
them all Pandars. Let all constant men be Troiluses, all false   85
women Cressids, and all brokers-between Pandars! Say "Amen."

TROILUS

Amen.

CRESSIDA

Amen.

PANDARUS

Amen. Whereupon I will show you a chamber, which bed,   90
because it shall not speak of your pretty encounters, press it to
death. Away!

MALE

He eats nothing but doves, and that breeds hot blood, and hot
blood begets hot thoughts, and hot thoughts beget hot deeds,
and hot deeds is love.   95

NARRATOR

Is this the generation of love? Hot blood, hot thoughts, and hot
deeds? Why they are vipers! Is love a generation of vipers?

[*Richard III*, I.ii]

ANNE

Poor key-cold figure of a holy king,   *key-cold*: as cold as a key
Pale ashes of the house of Lancaster,   (proverbial).
Thou bloodless remnant of that royal blood,
Be it lawful that I invocate thy ghost
To hear the lamentations of poor Anne,   5
Wife to thy Edward, to thy slaughtered son,
Stabbed by the selfsame hand that made these wounds!
Lo, in these windows that let forth thy life
I pour the helpless balm of my poor eyes.   *helpless*: useless.
O, cursed be the hand that made these holes!   10
Cursed the heart that had the heart to do it!
If ever he have wife, let her be made
More miserable by the life of him

Richard goes to the body and prevents the Narrator from entering the scene.

Anne crosses between the Narrator and Richard. The Narrator leaves the scene.

Anne shows Richard the body at her feet.

.

Than I am made by my young lord and thee!

RICHARD
Stay, you that bear the corpse, and set it down.

ANNE
Avaunt, thou dreadful minister of hell!
Thou hadst but power over his mortal body;
His soul thou canst not have. Therefore be gone.

RICHARD
Sweet saint, for charity, be not so curst.

ANNE
Foul devil, for God's sake, hence, and trouble us not,
For thou hast made the happy earth thy hell,
Filled it with cursing cries and deep exclaims.
If thou delight to view thy heinous deeds,
Behold this pattern of thy butcheries.

RICHARD
Lady, you know no rules of charity,
Which renders good for bad, blessings for curses.

ANNE
Villain, thou knowest nor law of God nor man.
No beast so fierce but knows some touch of pity.

RICHARD
But I know none, and therefore am no beast.

ANNE
O, wonderful, when devils tell the truth!

RICHARD
More wonderful, when angels are so angry.
Vouchsafe, divine perfection of a woman,
Of these supposed crimes to give me leave
By circumstance but to acquit myself.

ANNE
Vouchsafe, defused infection of a man,
Of these known evils but to give me leave
By circumstance to curse thy cursed self.

RICHARD
Fairer than tongue can name thee, let me have
Some patient leisure to excuse myself.

ANNE
Fouler than heart can think thee, thou canst make
No excuse current but to hang thyself.

RICHARD
By such despair I should accuse myself.

ANNE
And, by despairing, shouldst thou stand excused
For doing worthy vengeance on thyself
That didst unworthy slaughter upon others.

by: by the deaths of.

15

Avaunt: Go away.

curst: shrewish.

20
happy: naturally pleasant.
exclaims: exclamations.

Behold this pattern:
Look upon this example.
25

nor...nor:
neither...nor.

30

circumstance: detailed
explanation.
defused infection:
shapeless plague.

40
current: authentic
(a metaphor from coinage).

45

Anne tries to strike Richard. He stops her.

She turns back to the body. Richard moves behind Anne and holds her.

Richard lets go of Anne.

He circles Anne, looking at her admiringly.

RICHARD
Say that I slew them not.
ANNE
                         Then say they were not slain.
Didst thou not kill this king?
RICHARD
                     I grant ye.
ANNE
Dost grant me, hedgehog? Then God grant me too   50
Thou mayst be damned for that wicked deed.
O, he was gentle, mild, and virtuous!
RICHARD
The better for the King of Heaven that hath him.
ANNE
And thou unfit for any place but hell.
RICHARD
Yes, one place else—if you will hear me name it.   55
ANNE
Some dungeon.
RICHARD
          Your bedchamber.
ANNE
Ill rest betide the chamber where thou liest!
RICHARD
So will it, madam, till I lie with you.
ANNE
I hope so.   60
RICHARD
       I know so. But, gentle Lady Anne,
To leave this keen encounter of our wits
And fall something into a slower method,
Is not the causer of the timeless deaths   *timeless:* untimely.
Of these Plantagenets, Henry and Edward,   65
As blameful as the executioner?
ANNE
Thou art the cause and most accursed effect.   *effect:* effecting agent.
RICHARD
Your beauty was the cause of that effect—   *effect:* result.
Your beauty, which did haunt me in my sleep
To undertake the death of all the world,   70
So I might live one hour in your sweet bosom.   *So:* So that.
ANNE
If I thought that, I tell thee, homicide,   *homicide:* murderer.
These nails should rend that beauty from my cheeks.

50 hedgehog: a boar or wild hog was Richard's emblem.

Anne spits at Richard.

Richard pulls out a dagger and hands it to Anne as he speaks.

He kneels at her feet.

RICHARD
These eyes could not endure that beauty's wrack;
You should not blemish it if I stood by.
As all the world is cheered by the sun,
So I by that. It is my day, my life.
ANNE
Black night o'ershade thy day, and death thy life!
RICHARD
Curse not thyself, fair creature—thou art both.
ANNE
I would I were, to be revenged on thee.
RICHARD
It is a quarrel most unnatural
To be revenged on him that loveth thee.
ANNE
It is a quarrel just and reasonable
To be revenged on him that killed my husband.
RICHARD
He that bereft thee, lady, of thy husband,
Did it to help thee to a better husband.
ANNE
His better doth not breathe upon the earth.
RICHARD
He lives that loves thee better than he could.
ANNE
Where is he?
RICHARD
              Here. Why dost thou spit at me?
ANNE
Would it were mortal poison, for thy sake!
RICHARD
Never came poison from so sweet a place.
ANNE
Never hung poison on a fouler toad.
Out of my sight; thou dost infect mine eyes!
RICHARD
Thine eyes, sweet lady, have infected mine.
Those eyes of thine from mine have drawn salt tears.
Teach not thy lip such scorn, for it was made
For kissing, lady, not for such contempt.
If thy revengeful heart cannot forgive,
Lo, here I lend thee this sharp-pointed sword,
Which, if thou please to hide in this true breast
And let the soul forth that adoreth thee,
I lay it naked to the deadly stroke
And humbly beg the death upon my knee.

wrack: destruction.
75

both: i.e., night/day and death/life.
80

85

He lives: There is a man alive.

90

infected: i.e., with love.

100

He lays open his tunic; she begins to come at him with the dagger, then hesitates.
At each of his provoking words she raises her arm to stab him. When he speaks love to her, she arrests her impulse to kill him. She is dazed by his provocations and compliments.
She drops the sword.

Richard stays on the ground, the dagger poised at his heart.

He rises and puts the dagger aside.

He removes a ring from his finger.

He puts the ring on her finger.

Anne crosses upstage and remains standing; dazed, she does not appear to hear Richard's final speech. Richard speaks to the audience as he puts away his dagger.

Nay, do not pause; for I did kill King Henry—   105
But 'twas thy beauty that provoked me.
Nay, now dispatch; 'twas I that stabbed young Edward—
But 'twas thy heavenly face that set me on.
Take up the sword again or take up me.

ANNE
Arise, dissembler. Though I wish thy death,   110
I will not be thy executioner.

RICHARD
Then bid me kill myself, and I will do it.

ANNE
I have already.

RICHARD
           That was in thy rage.
Speak it again, and, even with the word,   115
This hand which, for thy love, did kill thy love,
Shall, for thy love, kill a far truer love.
To both their deaths shalt thou be accessory.   *accessory:* i.e., you share
                                                        the guilt.
ANNE
I would I knew thy heart.

RICHARD
'Tis figured in my tongue.   *figured:* displayed.

ANNE
I fear me both are false.

RICHARD
Then never man was true.

ANNE
Well, well, put up your sword.

RICHARD
Say, then, my peace is made.

ANNE
That shalt thou know hereafter.   125

RICHARD
But shall I live in hope?

ANNE
All men, I hope, live so.

RICHARD
Vouchsafe to wear this ring.

ANNE
To take is not to give.

RICHARD
Look how my ring encompasseth thy finger;   130
Even so thy breast encloseth my poor heart.
Wear both of them, for both of them are thine.
Was ever woman in this humor wooed?
Was ever woman in this humor won?

Two women watch Anne as she returns to the ensemble area.

The Narrator watches as Richard now begins to return to the ensemble area.

The Narrator moves away from the ensemble area and introduces the song.

All men repeat the last verse and direct it toward Katherine, princess of France, as she prepares to meet King Henry V.

I'll have her, but I will not keep her long. 135
What! I, that killed her husband and his father,
To take her in her heart's extremest hate,
With curses in her mouth, tears in her eyes,
The bleeding witness of my hatred by,

The bleeding witness:
The body of Henry.

Having God, her conscience, and these bars against me,
And I no friends to back my suit at all
But the plain Devil and dissembling looks?
And yet to win her! All the world to nothing!
Ha!

All the world to nothing:
Against extreme odds.

FIRST FEMALE
And if she did not hate him deadly, she would love him dearly. 145
SECOND FEMALE
Love is a familiar; love is a devil; there is no evil angel but love.
Even in the spring of love, thy love-springs rot? Shall love, in
building, grow so ruinous? Let the song be love. This love will
undo us all.

love-springs: tender, young
shoots of love.

["Who Is Silvia," from *Two Gentlemen of Verona,* IV.ii]

ALL VOICES
Who is Silvia? What is she,
    That all our swains commend her?
Holy, fair, and wise is she;
    The Heaven such grace did lend her,
That she might admired be.

admired: wondered at.

Is she kind as she is fair?
    For beauty lives with kindness;
Love doth to her eyes repair,
    To help him of his blindness,
And, being helped, inhabits there.

repair: pay a visit.

10

Then to Silvia let us sing,
    That Silvia is excelling;
She excells each mortal thing
    Upon the dull earth dwelling.
To her let us garlands bring.

15

NARRATOR
Now my thoughts and wishes bend toward our fertile France.

Katherine crosses downstage, then calls to Alice to help her prepare for the visit of the English king, Henry V. The scene generates a sense of urgency, as Katherine is attempting to learn as much English as possible prior to Henry's arrival. Unseen by the two women, Henry watches from the side of the stage.

[*Henry V*, III.iv]

KATHERINE
Alice, tu as été en Angleterre, et tu parles bien le language.

ALICE
Un peu, madame.

KATHERINE
Je te prie, m'enseignez. Il faut que j'apprenne à parler. Comment
appelez-vous la main en Anglois?

ALICE
La main? Elle est appelée de "hand."   5

KATHERINE
De "hand." Et les doigts?

ALICE
Les doigts? Ma foi, j'oublie les doigts! Mais je me souviendrai. Les
doigts? Je pense qu'ils sont appelés de "fingres." Oui, de "fingres."

KATHERINE
La main—de "hand"; les doigts—de "fingres." Je pense que je
suis le bon écolier; j'ai gagne deux mots d'Anglois vitement.   10
Comment appelez-vous les ongles?

ALICE
Les ongles? Nous les appelons de "nailès."

KATHERINE
De "nailès." Écoutez. Dites-moi si je parle bien: de "hand," de
"fingres," et de "nailès."

ALICE
C'est bien dit, madame; il est fort bon Anglois.   15

KATHERINE
Dites-moi l'Anglois pour le bras.

ALICE
De "arma," madame.

KATHERINE
Et le coude?

ALICE
"D'elbow."

1–12 KATHERINE: Alice, you have been in England, and you speak the
language well.
ALICE: A little, madam.
KATHERINE: Please teach me. I must learn to speak it. How do you say *la main* in English?
ALICE: *La main*? It is called de "hand."
KATHERINE: De "hand." And *les doigts*?
ALICE: *Les doigts*? By my faith, I forget *les doigts*. But I will remember. I think
that they are called de "fingres," yes, de "fingres."
KATHERINE: *La main*—de "hand"; *les doigts*—de "fingres." I think that I am a clever
pupil; I have learned two English words in no time. How do you say *les ongles*?
ALICE: *Les ongles*? We call them de "nailes."
13–25 KATHERINE: De "nailès." Listen. Tell me if I speak properly: de

Alice patiently corrects Katherine.

Katherine attempts to implant the word in her memory.

Alice compliments Katherine.

KATHERINE
D'elbow. Je m'en fais la répétition de tous les mots que vous   20
m'avez appris dès à présent.

ALICE
Il est trop difficile, madame, comme je pense.

KATHERINE
Excusez-moi, Alice, écoutez: de "hand," de "fingres," de "nailès,"
"d'arma," de "bilbow."

ALICE
De "elbow," madame.   25

KATHERINE
O, Seigneur Dieu! Je m'en oublie d'elbow. Comment appelez-
vous le col?

ALICE
De "neck," madame.

KATHERINE
De "nick." Et le menton?

ALICE
De "chin."   30

KATHERINE
De "sin." Le col—de "nick"; le menton—de "sin."

ALICE
Oui. Sauf votre honneur, en vérité, vous prononcez les mots aussi
droit ques les natifs d'Angleterre.

"hand," de "fingres," and de "nailès."
ALICE: That's quite correct, madame; it is very good English.
KATHERINE: Tell me the English for *le bras*.
ALICE: De "arma," madame.
KATHERINE: And *le coude*?
ALICE: "D'elbow."
KATHERINE: "D'elbow." I am going to repeat all the words that you have taught
me so far.
ALICE: It is too difficult, madame, I'm afraid.
KATHERINE: Pardon me, Alice, listen: de "hand," de "fingres," de "nailès," "d'arma,"
de "bilbow."
ALICE: "D'elbow," madame.
  26–40 KATHERINE: O Lord! I can't remember "d'elbow." How do you say *le col*?
ALICE: De "neck," madame.
KATHERINE: De "nick." And *le menton*?
ALICE: De "chin."
KATHERINE: De "sin." *Le col*—de "nick"; *le menton*—de "sin."
ALICE: Yes. If I may say so, in truth, you pronounce the words as well as a
native of England.
KATHERINE: I have no doubt that I will learn, with the help of God, and in a
very short time.
ALICE: Haven't you already forgotten what I've taught you?
KATHERINE: No, I shall recite for you at once: de "hand," de "fingres," de "mailès"…

Katherine, feeling very proud of herself, prances around the area.

Alice stops her.

Alice mouths the words as Katherine tries to remember them.

Alice loses some patience as she hears the same mistakes repeated.

Katherine asserts her royal self and pronounces the words.

Katherine giggles.

The women laugh together and play and dance with the words as Katherine repeats them.

King Henry is charmed by the women's playfulness. He strides up to them and interrupts them as they are talking and giggling.

Both women recoil in embarrassment at having been "caught" in the midst of their naughty foolery.

KATHERINE
Je ne doute point d'apprendre, par la grâce de Dieu, et en peu
de temps.   35
ALICE
N'avez-vous pas déjà oublié ce que je vous ai enseigné?
KATHERINE
Non, je réciterai à vous promptement: de "hand," de "fingres,"
de "mailès"...
ALICE
De "nailés," madame.
KATHERINE
De "nailès," de "arm," de "ilbow"...   40
ALICE
Sauf votre honneur, "d'elbow."
KATHERINE
Ainsi dis-je: "d'elbow," de "nick," et de "sin." Comment appelez-
vous le pied et la robe?
ALICE
Le "foot," madame, et le "count."
KATHERINE
Le "foot" et le "count"! O Seigneur Dieu! Ils sont les mots de son   45
mauvais—corruptible, gros, et impudique—et non pour les
dames de honneur d'user. Je ne voudrais prononcer ces mots de-
vant les seigneurs de France pour tout le monde. Foh! Le "foot"
et le "count"! Néanmoins, je réciterai une autre fois ma leçon ensemble:
de "hand," de "fingres," de "nailès," "d'arma," "d'elbow," de   50
"nick," de "sin," de "foot," le "count."
ALICE
Excellent, madame!

[*Henry V*, V.ii]

HENRY
                    Fair Katherine, and most fair,

ALICE: De "nailès," madame.
KATHERINE: De "nailès," de "arm," de "ilbow"...
  41–52 ALICE: Pardon me, "d'elbow."
KATHERINE: That's what I said: "d'elbow," de "nick," et de "sin." What do you
call *le pied* and *la robe*?
ALICE: Le "foot," madame, and le "count." [Alice's pronunciation makes "foot"
sound like the French word for "fornicate" (*foutre*) and "count" like the French
expression for "vagina."]
KATHERINE: O Lord! These are naughty words—wicked, gross, and immodest—and are not fit to be used by well-bred ladies. I couldn't say those words in
front of French gentlemen for all the world. Foh! Le "foot" and le "count"! Regardless, I
shall recite my entire lesson once more: de "hand," de "fingres," de "nailès," "d'arma,"
"d'elbow," de "nick," de "sin," de "foot," le "count."
ALICE: Excellent, madame!

Katherine attempts to repair her composure as Alice tries to fade into the background.

Katherine turns to Alice.

Katherine shares her suspicions with Alice.

Alice is fearful of acknowledging the correct translation.

Henry laughs.

Will you vouchsafe to teach a soldier terms   *terms:* words.
Such as will enter at a lady's ear
And plead his love-suit to her gentle heart?

KATHERINE
Your Majesty shall mock at me; I cannot speak your England.   5

HENRY
O fair Katherine, if you will love me soundly with your French
heart, I will be glad to hear you confess it brokenly with your
English tongue. Do you like me, Kate?

KATHERINE
Pardonnez-moi, I cannot tell wat is "like me."

HENRY
An angel is like you, Kate, and you are like an angel.   10

KATHERINE
Que dit-il? Que je suis semblable à les anges?

ALICE
Oui, vraiment, sauf votre grace, ainsi dit-il.

HENRY
I said so, dear Katherine, and I must not blush to affirm it.

KATHERINE
O bon Dieu! Les langues des hommes sont pleines de tromperies.

HENRY
What says she, fair one? That the tongues of men are full of deceits?   15

ALICE
Oui, zat de tongues of ze mans is be full of deceits. Zat is de Princess.

HENRY
The Princess is the better Englishwoman. I' faith, Kate, my wooing
is fit for thy understanding. I am glad thou canst speak no better
English, for, if thou couldst, thou wouldst think I had sold my
farm to buy my crown. I know no ways to mince it in love, but   20
directly to say "I love you." Then if you urge me farther than to
say "Do you in faith?" I wear out my suit. Give me your answer,
in faith, do. And so clap hands and a bargain. How say you, lady?   *clap:* clasp.

KATHERINE
Sauf votre honneur, me understand well.

HENRY
Marry, if you would put me to verses or to dance for your sake,   25
Kate, why you undid me. For the one, I have neither words nor
measure, and for the other, I have no strength in measure, yet a   *measure:* poetic meter.

11 Que...anges?: What does he say? That I am like the angels?

12 Oui...dit-il: Yes, truly, save your grace, so he says.

14 O bon Dieu...tromperies: translated by Henry in line 15.

17 the better Englishwoman: Like a true Englishwoman, the princess has a proper mistrust of flattery.

22 wear out my suit: fail in my wooing (with, perhaps, a pun on "wearing out the fabric of his suit of clothes" by spending too much time on his knees).

24 Sauf votre honneur: Save your honor.

Henry moves to take her hand.

Katherine tries to get away, but he holds both her hands.

Henry swings her around with joy.

Henry assumes a stance and prepares himself to speak French.

Katherine is touched by his valiant attempt at French.

Henry, feeling encouraged by her, attempts more eloquent phrases.

reasonable measure in strength. If I could win a lady at leapfrog, or by vaulting into my saddle with my armor on my back, under the correction of bragging be it spoken, I should quickly leap into a wife. But before God, Kate, I cannot look greenly nor gasp out of eloquence, nor I have no cunning in protestation—only downright oaths, which I never use till urged, nor never break for urging. If thou canst love a fellow of this temper, Kate, whose face is not worth sunburning, that never looks in his glass for love of anything he sees there, let thine eye be thy cook. I speak to thee plain soldier. If thou canst love me for this, take me; if not, to say to thee that I shall die is true—but for thy love, by the Lord, no! Yet I love thee too. If thou would have such a one, take me. And take me, take a soldier; take a soldier, take a king. And what sayest thou then to my love? Speak, my fair—and fairly, I pray thee.

KATHERINE

Is it possible zat I sould love de enemy of France?

HENRY

No, it is not possible you should love the enemy of France, Kate. But, in loving me, you should love the friend of France, for I love France so well that I will not part with a village of it. I will have it all mine. And, Kate, when France is mine and I am yours, then yours is France and you are mine.

KATHERINE

I cannot tell wat is zat.

HENRY

No, Kate? I will tell thee in French, which I am sure will hang upon my tongue like a new-married wife about her husband's neck, hardly to be shook off. Je quand sur le possession de France, et quand vous avez le possession de moi...let me see, what then? Saint Denis be my speed! Donc votre est France et vous êtes mienne. It is as easy for me, Kate, to conquer the kingdom as to speak so much more French. I shall never move thee in French, unless it be to laugh at me.

KATHERINE

Sauf votre honneur, le Francois que vous parlez, il est meilleur que l'Anglois lequel je parle.

HENRY

No, faith, is't not, Kate. How answer you, la plus belle Katherine du monde, mon tres cher et devin deesse?

measure...measure: dancing...amount of ability.
greenly: as if I were young and innocent.

glass: mirror.

And...soldier: if you take me, you also take a soldier.

45

50

Saint Denis: the patron saint of France.
55

60

34–35 not worth sunburning: i.e., because it is already so tanned and weather-beaten.

36 let thine eye be thy cook: your eye must "dress" me with good qualities just as your cook dresses meat prepared for your table.

51–52 a translation of the last sentence of Henry's speech.

57–58 Sauf...parle: Save your honor, your French is better than my English.

59–60 la...deesse: the most beautiful Katherine in the world, my very dear and divine goddess.

Katherine shares her compliment to Henry with Alice.

Henry pulls Katherine away from Alice.

Katherine curtsies to the king.

Katherine pulls her hand away and rushes from Henry in horror.

Alice curtsies to Henry.

Henry takes Katherine's hands.

KATHERINE
Your Majestee ave fausse French enough to deceive de most sage demoiselle zat is en France.

HENRY
Now, fie upon my false French! By mine honor, in true English, I love thee, Kate. Take me by the hand and say "Harry of England, I am thine." Which word thou shalt no sooner bless mine ear withal, but   65 I will tell thee aloud "England is thine, Ireland is thine, France is thine, and Henry Plantagenet is thine."

KATHERINE
Zat is as it sall please de roi mon pere.

HENRY
Nay, it will please him well, Kate; it shall please him, Kate.

KATHERINE
Zen it sall also content me.   70

HENRY
Upon that I kiss your hand, and I call you my Queen.

KATHERINE
Laissez, mon seigneur, laissez, laissez! Ma foi, je ne veux point que vous abaissiez votre grandeur en baisant la main d'une—Notre Seigneur!—indigne serviteur. Excusez-moi, je   75 vous supplie, mon très-puissant seigneur.

HENRY
Then I will kiss your lips, Kate.

KATHERINE
Les dames et demoiselles pour être baisées devant leur noces, il n'est pas la coutume de France.

HENRY
Madam my interpreter, what says she?

ALICE
Zat it is not be de fashion pour les ladies of France…I cannot   80 tell wat is "basier" en Anglish.

HENRY
To kiss.

ALICE
Your Majesty entendre better que moi.

HENRY
It is not a fashion for the maids in France to kiss before they are married, would she say?   85

ALICE
Oui, vraiment.

61 fausse: false, deceitful.
68 de roi mon pere: the king my father.
72–75 Laissez…seigneur: Don't, my lord, don't, don't! By my faith, I don't want you to lower your dignity by kissing the hand of an—Our Lord!—unworthy servant. Excuse me, I beg you, my most powerful lord.
77–78 Les dames…France: It is not the custom in France for ladies and young girls to be kissed before their weddings.
83 entendre better que moi: understands better than I.
86 Oui, vraiment: Yes, truly.

Henry embraces Katherine.

He kisses her. Alice returns to the ensemble area.

As Henry and Katherine return to their places in the ensemble area, the harmony of the wooing is interrupted by sudden doubts. Confusion breaks out among the others as each actor moves about the stage in search of help; some pass the Narrator and question him. Music underscores the unhappy atmosphere.

As the actors cross to their new places in the ensemble area, the following lines are spoken.

These lines are continually repeated till the Narrator turns to the audience and announces the following.

The ensemble now regroups in small clusters of people, as if friends were seeking the advice of other friends. The actor playing Launce leaves the group and enters the playing area with a basket of fruit. The Narrator turns his back on the emsemble and speaks to the audience.

The ensemble groups dissolve into earnest, troubled discussions among friends till Launce begins to speak to the audience.

HENRY

O Kate, nice customs curtsy to great kings. Dear Kate, you and I
cannot be confined within the weak list of a country's fashion.
We are the makers of manners, Kate, and the liberty that follows
our places stops the mouth of all find-faults—as I will do yours,
for upholding the nice fashion of your country in denying me a
kiss. Therefore, patiently and yielding. You have witchcraft in
your lips, Kate. There is more eloquence in a sugar touch of them than
in the tongues of the French council, and they should sooner persuade
Harry of England than a general petition of monarchs!   95

FEMALE

Beshrew that heart that makes my heart to groan
For that deep wound it gives my friend and me!

MALE

Is this her fault or mine?

FEMALE

I leave myself, my friends, and all for love.

MALE

All my powers do their bestowing lose.   100

FEMALE

My spirit grows heavy in love.

MALE

My love is a fever.

FEMALE

              Love is like a child
That longs for everything that he can come by.

NARRATOR

The course of true love never did run smooth.   105

NARRATOR

They that thrive well take counsel of their friends.

nice: foolish.
list: limit.
*the liberty that follows our
places:* the freedom that
comes with our high
rank.

Launce puts down his basket and pulls out a secret sheet of paper.

Speed enters quietly. He is curious about the paper which Launce has and he wishes to read it. In order to get the paper, he steals apples from Launce's basket and begins to juggle them.. Speed juggles close to Launce in order to read the paper. Launce tries to get back his apples, but when he feels Speed near, Launce quickly covers the paper.

Speed begins to pelt Launce with his apples; as Launce dodges, Speed snatches the paper out of his hand. Launce picks up the bruised apples and sadly returns them to his basket.

PART II
Seeking Advice About Love

[*Two Gentlemen of Verona*, III.i]

LAUNCE

I am but a fool, look you, and yet I am in love. But a team of horse shall not pluck that from me, nor who 'tis I love. And yet, 'tis a woman; but what woman, I will not tell myself. And yet, 'tis a maid; for she is her master's maid, and serves for wages. Here is the cate-log of her condition. "Imprimis: She can fetch and carry." Why, a horse can do no more. Nay, a horse cannot fetch, but only carry; therefore is she better than a jade.

SPEED

How now, Signior Launce? What news with your mastership?

LAUNCE

With my master's ship? Why it is at sea.

SPEED

Well, your old vice still: mistake the word. What news then in your paper?

LAUNCE

The blackest news that ever thou heardst.

SPEED

Why, man, how black?

LAUNCE

Why as black as ink.

SPEED

"Item: She can sew."

LAUNCE

That's as much as to say, "Can she so?"

SPEED

"Item: She can knit."

LAUNCE

What need a man care for a stock with a wench, when she can knit him a stock.

cate-log: Launce's pronunciation of "catalogue."
condition: qualities.
Imprimis: in the first place (generally followed by a list of items.) *jade:* horse (with a pun on "loose woman").
10

stock...stock: dowry ...stocking.

16 "Can she so?": sexually suggestive (perhaps accompanied by a lascivious gesture).

Much to Launce's chagrin, Speed tears the phrase out of the paper when Launce says "out with it." Launce retrieves the torn piece.

SPEED
"Item: She can wash and scour."   20

LAUNCE
A special virtue, for then she need not be washed and scoured.

SPEED
"Item: She can spin."

LAUNCE
Then may I set the world on wheels, when she can spin for her living.

set the world on wheels: live at ease. *spin for her living:* turn prostitute.

SPEED
"Item: She hath many nameless virtures."

nameless: unable to be named, inexpressible.

LAUNCE
That's as much as to say "bastard virtues," that indeed know not their fathers and therefore have no names.

SPEED
Here follow her vices.

LAUNCE
Close at the heels of her virtues.

SPEED
"Item: She is not to be kissed fasting, in respect of her breath."

in respect of: on account of.

LAUNCE
Well, that fault may be mended with a breakfast. Read on.   30

SPEED
"Item: She hath a sweet mouth."

sweet mouth: sweet tooth (with a bawdy pun intended).

LAUNCE
That makes amends for her sour breath.

SPEED
"Item: She doth talk in her sleep."

LAUNCE
It's no matter for that, so she sleep not in her talk.

SPEED
"Item: She is slow in words."   35

LAUNCE
O villain, that set this down among her vices! To be slow in words is a woman's only virtue. I pray thee, out with it, and place it for her chief virtue.

SPEED
"Item: She hath no teeth."

LAUNCE
I care not for that neither, because I love crusts.   40

SPEED
"Item: She is curst."

LAUNCE
Well, the best is, she hath no teeth to bite.

SPEED
"Item: She is too liberal."

liberal: free (lascivious).

34 so she sleep not in her talk: "sleep" puns on "slip," as both were pronounced similarly.

Speed speaks very slowly and exaggerates the words.

Speed tears the item out of the paper. Launce grabs this precious piece.

Launce lords his information over Speed.

Speed tears the letter in half and runs out.

Launce speaks to the Narrator as he collects the last piece of his treasured paper.

Launce follows Speed into the ensemble area. Lucetta and Julia cross to the acting area; Lucetta lags behind, following Julia with her eyes.

Lucetta gazes at Julia and speaks to the Narrator.

Male speaks to Narrator.

LAUNCE
Of her tongue she cannot, for that's writ down she is slow of; of
her purse she shall not, for that I'll keep shut. Now, of another   45
thing she may, and that cannot I help. Well, proceed.
SPEED
"Item: She hath more hair than wit, and more faults than hairs,
and more wealth than faults.
LAUNCE
Stop there—I'll have her! She was mine, and not mine, twice or
thrice in that last article. Rehearse that once more.   50
SPEED
"Item: She hath more hair than wit..."
LAUNCE
More hair than wit? It may be. What's next?
SPEED
"And more faults than hairs..."
LAUNCE
That's monstrous. O, that that were out!
SPEED
"And more wealth than faults."   55
LAUNCE
Why, that word makes the faults gracious. Well, I'll have her.   *gracious:* more easily
And if it be a match, as nothing is impossible—   accepted.
SPEED
What then?
LAUNCE
Why, then will I tell thee—that my master stays for thee at the   60
North-Gate.
SPEED
For me?
LAUNCE
For thee! Ay, who art thou? He hath stayed for a better man
than thee.
SPEED
Why didst not tell me sooner? Pox of your loveletters!
LAUNCE
Now will he be swinged for reading my letter—an unmannerly   *swinged:* thrashed.
slave, that will thrust himself into secrets.
LUCETTA
Is't not enough to torture me alone,
But slave to slavery my sweet'st friend must be!
MALE
                                    Thou dost advise me
Even so as I mine own course have set down.   70

45–46 another thing: the bawdy suggestion puns on the sexual connotation of "purse."

Lucetta joins Julia and begins to hem her skirt.

Lucetta hands Julia a letter after she bites the thread from the hem and puts away her needle.

Julia stamps her feet in anger.

Lucetta assumes a servant's attitude and curtsies to Julia.

[*Two Gentlemen of Verona*, I.ii]

JULIA
But say, Lucetta, now we are alone,
Wouldst thou then counsel me to fall in love?
LUCETTA
Ay, madame, so you stumble not unheedfully.
JULIA
What think'st thou of the gentle Proteus?
LUCETTA
Of many good I think him best.   5
JULIA
Your reason?
LUCETTA
I have no other but a woman's reason:
I think him so because I think him so.
JULIA
And wouldst thou have me cast my love on him?
LUCETTA
Ay, if you thought your love not cast away.   10
JULIA
Why he, of all the rest, hath never moved me.   *moved me:* proposed
LUCETTA   marriage to me.
Yet he, of all the rest, I think best loves ye.
JULIA
His little speaking shows his love but small.
LUCETTA
Fire that's closest kept burns most of all.
JULIA
They do not love that do not show their love.   15
LUCETTA
O, they love least that let men know their love.
JULIA
I would I knew his mind.
LUCETTA
Peruse this paper, madame.   *Peruse:* Read over.
JULIA
"To Julia." Say, from whom?
LUCETTA
That the contents will show.   20
JULIA
Say, say, who gave it thee?
LUCETTA
Sir Valentine's page; and sent, I think, from Proteus.
He would have given it you, but I being in the way,   *being in the way:* nearby.
Did in your name receive it. Pardon the fault, I pray.

Lucetta exits angrily. She does not go very far, but watches on the edge of the acting area, awaiting Julia's cry for help.

Lucetta returns immediately. When Julia sees her naughty pretence of servitude, she hides her impulsive excitement and curiosity.

As Lucetta starts to exit, she purposely drops the letter and elaborately picks it up and places it in her bosom.

Julia tries to get Lucetta to put the letter on the floor again.

Lucetta pulls out the letter and crosses to Julia to show it to her.

JULIA
Now, by my modesty, a goodly broker!
Dare you presume to harbor wanton lines?
To whisper and conspire against my youth?
There, take the paper. See it be returned,
Or else return no more into my sight.

broker: go-between.
harbor: conceal.

LUCETTA
To plead for love deserves more fee than hate.

more fee: better reimbursement.

JULIA
Will ye be gone?

LUCETTA
That you may ruminate.

ruminate: think things over.

JULIA
And yet I would I had o'erlooked the letter.
What ho! Lucetta!

o'erlooked: read over.

LUCETTA
What would your ladyship?

35

JULIA
Is't near dinnertime?

LUCETTA
I would it were,
That you might kill your stomach on your meat
And not upon your maid.

kill your stomach: (1) satisfy your appetite, (2) vent your irritation.
40

JULIA
What is't that you took up so gingerly.

LUCETTA
Nothing.

JULIA
Why didst thou stoop, then?

LUCETTA
To take a paper up that I let fall.

JULIA
And is that paper nothing?

LUCETTA
Nothing concerning me.

45

JULIA
Then let it lie for those that it concerns.

LUCETTA
Madam, it will not lie where it concerns
Unless it have a false interpreter.

concerns: is of importance to.
lie where it concerns: tell untruths in important matters.

JULIA
Some love of yours hath writ to you in rhyme.

LUCETTA
That I might sing it, madame, to a tune,

That: So that.

---

38 meat: with a pun on "mate" (Proteus) and "maid" (line 39).

Julia takes the letter out of Lucetta's hands and tears it into little pieces.

Lucetta exits.
Julia begins to pick up the pieces of the torn letter.

She throws down a fragment of the letter and steps upon it.

Julia puts the two pieces together as if they were paper dolls, kissing one another.
The Narrator watches Julia.
Julia picks up the remaining scraps of paper, kisses them, and returns to her place in the ensemble area.

The Narrator begins to move toward the Male, when Claudio and Benedick come jogging in with towels around their necks. Seeing them engaged in conversation, the Narrator stops and speaks.

Give me a note; your ladyship can set.

JULIA
As little by such toys as may be possible.
Go get you gone, and let the papers lie;
You would be fingering them to anger me.

LUCETTA
She makes it strange, but she would be best pleased
To be so angered with another letter.

JULIA
Nay, would I were so angered with the same!
O hateful hands, to tear such loving words!
Injurious wasps, to feed on such sweet honey
And kill the bees that yield it with your stings!
I'll kiss each several paper for amends.
Look, here is writ "kind Julia." Unkind Julia!
As in revenge of thy ingratitude,
I throw thy name against the bruising stones,
Trampling contemptuously on thy disdain.
And here is writ "love-wounded Proteus."
Poor wounded name! My bosom as a bed
Shall lodge thee till thy wound be throughly healed;
And thus I search it with a sovereign kiss.
But twice or thrice was "Proteus" written down.
Be calm, good wind; blow not a word away
Till I have found each letter in the letter,
Except mine own name. That some whirlwind bear
Unto a ragged, fearful-hanging rock,
And throw it thence into the raging sea!
Lo, here in one line is his name twice writ:
"Poor, forlorn Proteus, passionate Proteus,
To the sweet Julia." That I'll tear away.
And yet I will not, sith so prettily
He couples it to his complaining names.
Thus will I fold them, one upon another.
Now kiss, embrace, contend—do what you will.

NARRATOR
It is the prettiest villain!

MALE
O, never say that I was false at heart,
Though absence seemed my flame to qualify.

NARRATOR
He wants advice!
What, a play toward? I'll be an auditor;
And actor too, perhaps, if I see cause.

---

note: (1) musical note, (2) Proteus's letter.
toys: trifles.

fingering: playing with.

makes it strange: pretends to be indifferent.

Nay…same!: I wish I still had the untorn letter to be angry about. *wasps:* i.e., her fingers.
each several paper: each separate piece of paper.
Unkind: Unnatural.
As: As if.
65

search: cleanse (as if the name were wounded).
sovereign: restorative.

75

sith: since. *prettily:* honestly (without guile or deceit).
complaining: lamenting.

85

---

51 set: (1) set to music, (2) write. Julia takes the word in the sense of "setting" a value on something.

Claudio and Benedick are exercising as if in a gym or men's locker room. There is an edge of competition between them as they do sit-ups or push-ups.

Claudio stops Benedick from continuing the exercises.

[*Much Ado about Nothing*, I.i]

CLAUDIO
Benedick, didst thou note the daughter of Signior Leonato?

note: pay special attention to.

BENEDICK
I noted her not, but I looked on her.

CLAUDIO
Is she not a modest young lady?

BENEDICK
Do you question me, as an honest man should do, for my simple, true judgment? Or would you have me speak after my custom, as being a professed tyrant to their sex?

5

tyrant: someone who is cruel or heartless.
sober: serious.

CLAUDIO
No, I pray thee speak in sober judgment.

BENEDICK
Why, in faith, methinks she's too low for a high praise, too brown for a fair praise, and too little for a great praise. Only this commendation I can afford her: That were she other than she is, she were unhandsome; and being no other but as she is, I do not like her.

low: short.
fair: (1) just, (2) beautiful, (3) of light complexion.

CLAUDIO
Thou thinkest I am in sport. I pray thee, tell me truly how thou likest her.

BENEDICK
Would you buy her, that you inquire after her?

15

CLAUDIO
Can the world buy such a jewel?

BENEDICK
Yes, and a case to put it into.

case: (1) jewel box, (2) clothes, outer garments, (3) vagina (?).

CLAUDIO
In mine eye, she is the sweetest lady that ever I looked on.

BENEDICK
I can see yet without spectacles, and I see no such matter. There's her cousin, an she were not possessed with a fury, exceeds her as much in beauty as the first of May doth the last of December. But I hope you have no intent to turn husband, have you?

an: who, if.

CLAUDIO
I would scarce trust myself, though I had sworn the contrary, if Hero would be my wife.

BENEDICK
Is it come to this? In faith, hath not the world one man but he will wear his cap with suspicion? Shall I never see a bachelor of threescore again? Go to, in faith! And thou wilt needs thrust thy neck into a yoke, wear the print of it and sigh away Sundays.

25

26 wear his cap with suspicion: i.e., to conceal his cuckold's horns.
28 sigh away Sundays: men were expected to spend Sundays with their wives.

The Narrator (with a towel in his hands, as if returning from exercise) joins the men and assumes the role of Don Pedro.

Benedick begins jogging in place.

Look, Don Pedro is returned to seek you.

DON PEDRO

What secret hath held you here, that you followed not to Leonato's?   30

BENEDICK

He is in love! With who? Mark how short his answer is: with
Hero, Leonato's short daughter.

CLAUDIO

If my passion change not shortly, God forbid it should be otherwise.

DON PEDRO

Amen, if you love her; for the lady is very well worthy.

CLAUDIO

You speak this to fetch me in, my lord.   35

DON PEDRO

By my troth, I speak my thought.

CLAUDIO

And in faith, my lord, I spoke mine.

BENEDICK

And, by my two faiths and troths, my lord, I spoke mine.

CLAUDIO

That I love her, I feel.

DON PEDRO

That she is worthy, I know.

BENEDICK

That I neither feel how she should be loved, nor know how she
should be worthy, is the opinion that fire cannot melt out of me.
I will die in it at the stake.

DON PEDRO

Thou wast ever an obstinate heretic in the despite of beauty.   *despite:* contempt.

CLAUDIO

And never could maintain his part but in the force of his will.

BENEDICK

That a woman conceived me, I thank her; that she brought me
up, I likewise give her most humble thanks. But that I will have a
rechate winded in my forehead, all women shall pardon me.
Because I will not do them the wrong to mistrust any, I will do
myself the right to trust none; and the fine is, for the which I may   *fine:* conclusion.
go the finer, I will live a bachelor.   *go the finer:* spend more

DON PEDRO   money on clothes.

I shall see thee, ere I die, look pale with love.

35 to fetch me in: to trick me into revealing my true thoughts.

45 the force of his will: i.e., as opposed to using reason as a guide (Claudio's reply puns on the word "heretic" in line 44).

47–48 a rechate winded in my forehead: a "rechate" was a series of notes blown ("winded") on a horn to call the
hounds together during a hunt. The allusion, once again, is to the cuckold's horns which grew out of a man's forehead
and which signified a wife's unfaithfulness.

Benedick runs out, and Claudio runs behind attempting to catch up.

The Narrator / Don Pedro calls these final lines out to Benedick as Rosalind and Celia enter the playing area.

Rosalind is dressing herself as a boy with Celia's help. The Narrator, standing nearby, assists by continually taking away Rosalind's old clothes and handing Celia new ones. The women do not need to acknowledge the Narrator's presence as anything more than a prop person or "clothes rack."

BENEDICK
With anger, with sickness, or with hunger, my lord—not with love.
DON PEDRO
Well, if ever thou dost fall from this faith, thou wilt prove a
notable argument.

notable argument: a lively
subject for future
conversation.

[*As You Like It*, III.iv]

ROSALIND
Never talk to me! I will weep!
CELIA
Do, I prithee, but yet have the grace to consider that tears do not
become a man.
ROSALIND
But have I not cause to weep?
CELIA
As good cause as one would desire; therefore weep.   5
ROSALIND
His very hair is of the dissembling color.
CELIA
Something browner than Judas's. Marry, his kisses are Judas's
own children.
ROSALIND
In faith, his hair is of a good color.
CELIA
An excellent color—your chestnut was ever the only color.
ROSALIND
And his kissing is as full of sanctity as the touch of holy bread.
CELIA
He hath bought a pair of cast lips of Diana. A nun of winter's
sisterhood kisses not more religiously; the very ice of chastity is
in them.
ROSALIND
But why did he swear he would come this morning and comes not?
CELIA
Nay, certainly, there is no truth in him.
ROSALIND
Do you think so?
CELIA
Yes. I think he is not a pick-purse nor a horsestealer; but for his
verity in love, I do think him as concave as a covered goblet or
a worm-eaten nut.

your chestnut: this chestnut
color (indefinite expression).
holy bread: communion
bread blessed in the church.
cast: cast off, discarded by.
Diana: goddess of chastity
and the hunt. *of winter's
sisterhood:* devoted to the
cold, wintery virtue of
chastity.

verity: truthfulness. *concave:*
hollow. *covered goblet:* an

---

6 the dissembling color: according to tradition, Judas's hair was reddish.
7–8 Judas's own children: false, traitorous (like their father, who betrayed Christ).

Rosalind and Celia remain in the playing area. Rosalind affects a manly pose as a Male approaches the Narrator.

As the Narrator begins to answer, Romeo enters the playing area. Celia, Rosalind (stamping her feet like a big man in boots), and the Male cross to the periphery of the playing area. Seeing how downcast Romeo looks, the Narrator assumes the role of Benvolio and addresses him.

Romeo turns away from the Narrator, but remains in the playing area.
A man and woman enter the stage and speak to the Narrator.

The Narrator shrugs, then turns away from the two petitioners.
He is immediately met by Silvius, who takes his arm.

ROSALIND
Not true in love?

CELIA
Yes, when he is in; but I think he is not in.

ROSALIND
You have heard him swear downright he was.

CELIA
"Was" is not "is." O, that's a brave man! He writes brave verses, speaks brave words, swears brave oaths, and breaks them brave-ly athwart the heart of his lover. But all's brave that youth mounts and folly guides. Who comes here?

MALE
You are a counselor; you can command these elements to silence and work the peace of the present. Use your authority.

empty cup (which would have been kept covered when not in use).

brave: excellent (with a sense of irony).

[*Romeo and Juliet,* I.i]

NARRATOR
Good morrow, cousin.

ROMEO
                  Is the day so young?

NARRATOR
But new struck nine.

ROMEO
               Ay me, sad hours seem long!

NARRATOR
What sadness lengthens Romeo's hours?   5

ROMEO
Not having that which, having, makes them short.

NARRATOR
In love?

ROMEO
Out.

NARRATOR
Of love?

ROMEO
Out of her favor, where I am in love.   10

FEMALE
Give me some counsel.

FIRST MALE
As thou art a gentleman of blood, advise me.

SECOND MALE
We will all subscribe to thy advice.

SILVIUS
O Corin, that thou knew'st how I do love her!

Another Male enters the acting area and begins to sing to the Narrator and the others present. Gradually, during the song, the remaining two women in the ensemble move into the acting area.

Now all the actors surround the Narrator in the playing area. They are dejected; Love has been unkind, and the Narrator has been no help in solving their problems. The following lines are delivered by separate groups of actors. Rosalind speaks to Celia.
Troilus talks to another Male.

The Narrator moves among the members of the group, trying to explain.
They do not listen to him; they continue complaining to one another.

NARRATOR
I partly guess, for I have loved ere now.   15
SILVIUS
O, if thy love were ever like to mine—
As sure, I think, did never man love so—
How many actions most ridiculous
Hast thou been drawn to by thy fantasy?
NARRATOR
Into a thousand that I have forgotten.   20
SILIVUS
O, thou didst then never love so heartily!
If thou rememb'rest not the slightest folly
That ever love did make thee run into,
Thou hast not loved;
Or if thou hast not sat as I do now,   25
Wearing thy hearer in thy mistress' praise,   *Wearing:* Wearying.
Thou hast not loved;
Or if thou hast not broke from company
Abruptly, as my passion now makes me,
Thou hast not loved.   30

["When Griping Griefs," from *Romeo and Juliet*, IV.v]

MALE
When griping griefs the heart doth wound,
    And doleful dumps the mind oppress,
    Then music with her silver sound
With speedy help doth lend redress.
ROSALIND
O coz, coz, coz, my pretty little coz, that thou didst know how   35
many fathom deep I am in love! But it cannot be sounded; my af-
fection hath an unknown bottom, like the Bay of Portugal.
TROILUS
Even such a passion doth embrace my bosom.
My heart beats thicker than a feverish pulse,   *thicker:* stronger.
And all my powers do their bestowing lose.   40
NARRATOR
He would embrace no counsel, take no warning.
ANGELO
What's this, what's this? Is this her fault or mine?
The tempter or the tempted—who sins most?
MALE
Th'expedition of my violent love   *expedition:* haste.

72

The Narrator tries to calm the group's unhappy mood.

Everyone begins to exit. Above a general muttering sound, the following lines may be heard.

On this last line, the narrator is left alone on the stage as the lights fade.

Out run the pauser, reason.   45
NARRATOR
Not so hot!
MALE
We need no more of your advice.
FIRST FEMALE
Love and fortune be my gods, my guide!
FIRST MALE
Reason and love keep little company together nowadays.
SECOND FEMALE
I leave myself, my friends, and all for love!   50
SECOND MALE
I love and hate her.
THIRD MALE
Fie, no more of love!

End of Act One

ACT II

Benedick enters the stage alone and speaks directly to the audience.

PART I
Having Problems with Love

BENEDICK

I do much wonder that one man, seeing how much another man is a fool when he dedicates his behaviors to love, will, after he hath laughed at such shallow follies in others, become the argument of his own scorn by falling in love. And such a man is Claudio! I have known when there was no music with him but the drum and the fife; and now had he rather hear the tabor and the pipe. I have known when he would have walked ten mile afoot to see a good armor, and now he will lie ten nights awake carving the fashion of a new doublet. He was wont to speak plain and to the purpose, like an honest man and a soldier, and now is he turned orthography—his words are a very fantastical banquet, just so many strange dishes. May I be so converted and see with these eyes? I cannot tell. I think not. I will not be sworn but love may transform me into an oyster; but I'll take my oath on it: Till he have made an oyster of me, he shall never make me such a fool. One woman is fair, yet I am well; another is wise, yet I am well; another virtuous, yet I am well; but till all graces be in one woman, one woman shall not come in my grace. Rich she shall be, that's certain; wise, or I'll none; virtuous, or I'll never cheapen her; fair, or I'll never look on her; mild, or come not near me; noble, or not I for an angel; of good discourse, an excellent musician, and her hair shall be of what color it please God. Ha!

argument: topic.

5

drum and the fife: instruments of war. *tabor and the pipe:* instruments of peace (a "tabor" was a small drum). *armor:* suit of armor. *carving:* imagining, planning. *He was wont:* It was his fashion. *turned orthography:* talks only in fashionable phrases.

grace: i.e., be pleasing to me. *I'll none:* I won't have her. *cheapen:* bargain for her.

21 angel: a ten-shilling coin (pun on "noble," a coin worth six shillings eight pence).
22 hair...God: if she fulfills all these other requirements, I don't care what color her hair is.

Benedick is returning to the ensemble area when Beatrice enters and speaks to him.

Beatrice turns on her heels and crosses away from Benedick as if to leave.

Benedick crosses out and passes her by as he returns to the ensemble area.

The ensemble now enter singly, in pairs, and in small groups; they are unhappy—more troubled than at the close of act I. The women take positions on the stage completely separate from the men, as if they represent two armed camps.
The ensemble speak to one another or to images that they are conjuring up in their minds.

[*Much Ado about Nothing*, I.i]

BEATRICE
I wonder that you will still be talking, Signior Benedick. Nobody
marks you.

still: always.
marks: listens to.

BENEDICK
What, my dear Lady Disdain! Are you yet living?

BEATRICE
Is it possible Disdain should die while she hath such meet food to
feed it as Signior Benedick? Courtesy must convert to Disdain if
you come in her presence.

convert: change.

BENEDICK
Then is Courtesy a turncoat. But it is certain I am loved of all
ladies—only you excepted—and I would I could find in my heart
that I had not a hard heart, for truly I love none.

BEATRICE
A dear happiness to women! They would else have been troubled with a pernicious suitor. I thank God and my cold blood; I
am of your humor for that. I had rather hear my dog bark at a
crow than a man swear he loves me.

A dear happiness: Excellent
good luck.

BENEDICK
God keep your ladyship still in that mind. So some gentleman or
other shall scape a predestinate scratched face.

scape a predestinate: escape
an inevitable (the reward of
anyone who marries
Beatrice). *were:* is.

BEATRICE
Scratching could not make it worse, and 'twere such a face as
yours were.

BENEDICK
Well, you are a rare parrot-teacher.

BEATRICE
A bird of my tongue is better than a beast of yours.

A bird...yours: A
bird taught to speak as I
do is better than a beast
which speaks as you do.
continuer: i.e., with such
endurance.

BENEDICK
I would my horse had the speed of your tongue, and so good a
continuer. But keep your way, in God's name. I have done.

MALE TO FEMALE
Is it thy will thy image should keep open
My heavy eyelids to the weary night?

FEMALE
Poor lady; she were better love a dream.

MALE
My love is a fever.

25

FEMALE
Straight on kisses dream.

MALE
He is in love.

---

18 parrot-teacher: you would be a good teacher of parrots because you repeat the same words over and over.

The Narrator, looking at the male and female "camps," turns to the audience.

Phebe is pursued by Silvius; the Narrator watches.

After chasing Phebe for two or three rounds in the playing area, Silvius runs in front of her to stop her flight.

Silvius drops to his knees.

MALE
If love be rough with you, be rough with love.
MALE
I will be horribly in love with her.
FEMALE
Love can comment upon every woe.   30
MALE
I love and hate her.
MALE
My spirit grows heavy in love.
MALE
Fie, no more of love!
NARRATOR
It is as easy to count atomies as to resolve the propositions of a lover.
VOICES
Death-marked love
Erring love
Cunning love
NARRATOR
Love like a shadow flies when substance love pursues,
Pursuing that that flies, and flying what pursues.

atomies: atoms, small
particles. *propositions:*
questions.

[*As You Like It*, III.v]

SILVIUS
Sweet Phebe, do not scorn me! Do not, Phebe!
Say that you love me not, but say not so
In bitterness. The common executioner,
Whose heart the accustomed sight of death makes hard,
Falls not the axe upon the humbled neck
But first begs pardon. Will you sterner be
Than he that dies and lives by bloody drops?
PHEBE
I would not be thy executioner.
I fly thee, for I would not injure thee.
Thou tellest me there is murder in mine eye.
'Tis pretty, sure, and very probable
That eyes, that are the frailest and softest things,
Who shut their coward gates on atomies,
Should be called tyrants, butchers, murderers!
Now I do frown on thee with all my heart,
And if mine eyes can wound, now let them kill thee.
Now counterfeit to swoon; why, now fall down.
Or, if thou canst not, O, for shame, for shame,
Lie not to say mine eyes are murderers.

falls: lets fall.
But first begs: Without first
begging. *dies and lives:*
makes his living by causing
the deaths of other people.
for: because.
10
pretty: clever, witty.
sure: surely.
Who...atomies:
Which shut their lids to
keep out small particles.

counterfeit: pretend.

Rosalind and Celia become interested in the scene and stand on the periphery of the action.

Rosalind comes forward in her manly clothes.

Rosalind addresses Phebe.

Rosalind turns to Celia occasionaly to share her scorn.

Rosalind talks to Silvius.

Rosalind thoroughly enjoys being in command of this situation.

Now show the wound mine eye hath made in thee.　20
Scratch thee but with a pin, and there remains
Some scar of it. But now mine eyes,
Which I have darted at thee, hurt thee not;
Nor, I am sure, there is no force in eyes
That can do hurt.　25

SILVIUS

　　　　　　　O dear Phebe,
If ever—as that ever may be near—
You meet in some fresh cheek the power of fancy,　*fresh:* young. *fancy:* love.
Then shall you know the wounds invisible
That love's keen arrows make.　30

PHEBE

　　　　　　　　　But till that time
Come not thou near me; and when that time comes,
Afflict me with thy mocks; pity me not,　*mocks:* ridicule.
As till that time I shall not pity thee.

ROSALIND

And why, I pray you? Who might be your mother　35
That you insult, exult, and all at once,　*all at once:* in a single
Over the wretched? What though you have no beauty—　breath. *no:* no more.
As, by my faith, I see no more in you
Than without candle may go dark to bed—
Must you be therefore proud and pitiless?　40
Why, what means this? Why do you look on me?
I see no more in you than in the ordinary　*ordinary:* common
Of nature's sale-work. 'Od's my little life,　production. *Of nature's sale-*
I think she means to tangle my eyes too!　*work:* Of the humblest
No, faith, proud mistress; hope not after it.　products of nature. *'Od's:*
'Tis not your inky brows, your black silk hair,　God save. *tangle:* entangle
Your bugle eyeballs, nor your cheek of cream　(by love's design). *cream:*
That can entame my spirits to your worship.　cream-colored. *entame:* sub-
You, foolish shepherd, wherefore do you follow her,　due. *your worship:* worship
Like foggy south, puffing with wind and rain?　of you. *south:* the South
You are a thousand times a properer man　Wind. *wind and rain:* the
Than she a woman. 'Tis such fools as you　sighs and tears of Silvius.
That makes the world full of ill-favored children.
'Tis not her glass, but you that flatters her,　*glass:* mirror.
And out of you she sees herself more proper　*out of you:* with you
Than any of her lineaments can show her.　serving as her mirror.
But, mistress, know yourself. Down on your knees　*lineaments:* features
And thank heaven, fasting, for a good man's love;　(physical characteristics).
For I must tell you friendly in your ear:　*friendly:* as a friend.

38–39 I...bed: i.e., you are not beautiful enough to brighten up the darkness.
47 bugle: shiny and black (a "bugle" was a rounded, black glass bead used for decoration).

Rosalind starts to exit with Celia.

Phebe grabs Rosalind by the arm.

To Phebe.
To Silvius

Rosalind shares her fun with Celia.

Rosalind grabs Silvius by the arm and pushes him toward Phebe. Rosalind exits with Celia.

Sell when you can; you are not for all markets.
Cry the man mercy; love him; take his offer.
Foul is most foul, being foul to be a scoffer.
So take her to thee, shepherd. Fare you well.

PHEBE
Sweet youth, I pray you, chide a year together.
I had rather hear you chide than this man woo.

ROSALIND
He's fallen in love with your foulness, and she'll fall in love with
my anger. If it be so, as fast as she answers thee with frowning looks,
I'll sauce her with bitter words. Why look you so upon me?

PHEBE
For no ill will I bear you.

ROSALIND
I pray you, do not fall in love with me.
For I am falser than vows made in wine.
Besides, I like you not. Shepherd, ply her hard.
Come, come! Shepherdess, look on him better,
And be not proud. Though all the world could see,
None could be so abused in sight as he.

SILVIUS
Sweet Phebe...

PHEBE
                    Ha, what sayest thou, Silvius?

SILVIUS
Sweet Phebe, pity me.

PHEBE
Why, I am sorry for thee, gentle Silvius.

SILVIUS
Wherever sorrow is, relief would be.
If you do sorrow at my grief in love,
By giving love, your sorrow and my grief
Were both extermined.

PHEBE
Thou hast my love. Is not that neighborly?

SILVIUS
I would have you.

PHEBE
                    Why, that were covetousness.
Silvius, the time was that I hated thee.
And yet it is not that I bear thee love,
But since that thou canst talk of love so well,
Thy company, which erst was irksome to me,
I will endure, and I'll employ thee too.

60
Cry the man mercy: Beg his pardon. *Foul...scoffer:* An ugly woman seems at her worst when she rejects love.
together: continuously.

sauce: rebuke.

could see: could look at you. *abused in sight:* deceived by his eyes.

Wherever...be: When sorrow visits someone, relief is sure to follow.
Were both extermined: Would both be banished at the same time.

85

And yet it is not: i.e., the time has not yet come.
erst: before.

---

84 neighborly: i.e., I love you as a good Christian neighbor should (but not as you want me to love you).

86 covetousness: the reference to the tenth commandment implies that Silvius is sinning by breaking God's law (Phebe also plays on the Christian associations of the word "neighborly" above).

Silvius sinks to his knees again.

Phebe sits beside Silvius.

Phebe turns all of her persuasive charm on Silvius.

But do not look for future recompense
Than thine own gladness that thou art employed.
SILVIUS
So holy and so perfect is my love,
And I in such a poverty of grace,
That I shall think it a most plenteous crop
To glean the broken ears after the man
That the main harvest reaps. Loose now and then
A scattered smile, and that I'll live upon.
PHEBE
Knowest thou the youth that spoke to me erewhile?
SILVIUS
Not very well, but I have met him oft.
PHEBE
Think not I love him, though I ask for him.
'Tis but a peevish boy, yet he talks well.
But what care I for words? Yet words do well.
When he that speaks them pleases those that hear.
It is a pretty youth—not very pretty—
But, sure, he's proud, and yet his pride becomes him;
He'll make a proper man. The best thing in him
Is his complexion; and, faster than his tongue
Did make offense, his eye did heal it up.
He is not very tall, yet for his years he's tall.
His leg is but so-so, and yet 'tis well.
There was a pretty redness in his lip,
A little riper and more lusty red.
Than that mixed in his cheek; 'twas just the difference
Betwixt the constant red and mingled damask.
There be some women, Silvius, had they marked him
In parcels, as I did, would have gone near
To fall in love with him; but, for my part,
I love him not nor hate him not; and yet,
I have more cause to hate him than to love him.
For what had he to do to chide at me?
He said mine eyes were black and my hair black,
And, now I am remembered, scorned at me.
I marvel why I answered not again.
But that's all one; omittance is no quittance.
I'll write to him a very taunting letter,
And thou shalt bear it. Wilt thou, Silvius?

poverty of grace: scarceness of good favor.
ears: ears of corn.
Loose…smile: the metaphor, from archery, means to let arrows fly at will in a random pattern.
erewhile: earlier

105

110

115
constant: of uniform color.
mingled damask: mixed red and white. *marked… parcels:* paid attention to him part by part.

For…do: What business did he have.
I am remembered: I remember.

126 omittance is no quittance: a legal proverb meaning "I am still able to reply."

Phebe leads Silvius back to the ensemble area; the Narrator watches them depart.

The Narrator gestures toward Silvius.

The Hero-Claudio wedding party begins to assemble. Two women in the ensemble place Hero's veil on her head and hand her a bouquet. They send her off to the playing area with her father, Leonato, at her side while the women stay behind. The Musician plays the Wedding March as Hero and Leonato join Claudio and his best man, Benedick, before the Friar.

Taking the role of Don Pedro, the Narrator joins the wedding party.

Hero is the only woman in the playing area. She is surrounded by men; at one side is her intended bridegroom, Claudio, at the other side and a few steps behind is her father, Leonato. To Leonato's side is Don Pedro (Narrator), and to the bridegroom's side and slightly behind is his best man, Benedick. The Priest is in front. The Friar addresses Claudio.

SILVIUS
Phebe, with all my heart!
NARRATOR
One that loved not wisely but too well.   130
MALE
Is love a tender thing? It is too rough,
Too rude, too boisterous, and it pricks like a thorn.
FEMALE
Sorrow on love hereafter shall attend;
It shall be waited on with jealously,   *with:* by.
Find sweet beginning, but unsavory end.   135
NARRATOR
O, how this spring of love resembleth
The uncertain glory of an April day,
Which now shows all the beauty of the sun,
And by and by a cloud takes all away.

[*Much Ado about Nothing*, IV.i]

LEONATO
Come, Friar Francis, be brief—only to the plain form of mar-
riage, and you shall recount their particular duties afterwards.
FRIAR
You come hither, my lord, to marry this lady.
CLAUDIO
No.
LEONATO
To be married to her. Friar, you come to marry her.   5
FRIAR
Lady, you come hither to be married to this Count.
HERO
I do.
FRIAR
If either of you know any inward impediment why you should   *inward:* secret.
not be conjoined, I charge you, on your souls, to utter it.
CLAUDIO
Know you any, Hero?   10
HERO
None, my lord.
FRIAR
Know you any, Count?
LEONATO
I dare make his answer: none.
CLAUDIO
O, what men dare do! What men may do! What men daily do,
not knowing what they do!   15

Claudio pushes the Priest out of the way.

Here Claudio pushes Hero toward Leonato. The effect should seem as if she were an object being passed back and forth between two men.

BENEDICK
How now? Interjections? Why, then, some be of laughing, as
"ah, ha, he!"
CLAUDIO
Stand thee by, Friar. Father, by your leave,
Will you with free and unconstrained soul
Give me this maid, your daughter?   20
LEONATO
As freely, son, as God did give her me.
CLAUDIO
And what have I to give you back, whose worth
May counterpoise this rich and precious gift?   *counterpoise:* equal.
LEONATO
Nothing, unless you render her again.
CLAUDIO
Sweet Prince, you learn me noble thankfulness.   *learn:* teach.
There, Leonato, take her back again.
Give not this rotten orange to your friend:
She's but the sign and semblance of her honor.
Behold how like a maid she blushes here!
O, what authority and show of truth   *authority:* calm assurance.
Can cunning sin cover itself withal!
Comes not that blood as modest evidence   *that blood:* i.e., the blood
To witness simple virtue? Would you not swear,   rising in her cheeks. *modest*
All you that see her, that she were a maid,   *evidence:* proof of her
By these exterior shows? But she is none!   modesty. *witness:* bear
She knows the heat of a luxurious bed;   witness to. *shows:* signs.
Her blush is guiltiness, not modesty.   *luxurious:* lustful.
LEONATO
What do you mean, my lord?
CLAUDIO
                    Not to be married,
Not to knit my soul to an approved wanton.   *approved:* proved.
LEONATO
Dear my lord, if you, in your own proof,   *in your own proof:* in an
Have vanquished the resistence of her youth   attempt to prove her
And made defeat of her virginity...   chastity.
CLAUDIO
I know what you would say: If I have known her,
You will say she did embrace me as a husband,   45
And so extenuate the 'forehand sin.   *extenuate:* diminish (and,
No, Leonato,   therefore, excuse). *the*

16–17 How...he!": Interjections were often classified in Renaissance grammar texts according to their emotional
context; Benedick's example is quoted from John Lyly's Latin grammar.

Benedick attempts to stop Claudio. Claudio rejects him. The Friar quietly exits the area so as not to draw attention to his retreat.

Claudio moves close to Hero to touch her face. He pulls his hand away in disgust.

I never tempted her with word too large,
But, as a brother to his sister, showed
Bashful sincerity and comely love.

HERO
And seemed I ever otherwise to you?

CLAUDIO
Out on thee! Seeming! I will write against it.
You seem to me as Dian in her orb,
As chaste as is the bud ere it be blown.
But you are more intemperate in your blood
Than Venus, or those pampered animals
That rage in savage sensuality.

HERO
Is my lord well, that he doth speak so wide?

BENEDICK
This looks not like a nuptial.

HERO
                    True! O God!

CLAUDIO
Let me but move one question to your daughter;
And by that fatherly and kindly power
That you have in her, bid her answer truly.

LEONATO
I charge thee do so, as thou art my child.

HERO
O, God defend me! How am I beset!
What kind of catechizing call you this?

CLAUDIO
To make you answer truly to your name.

HERO
Is it not "Hero"? Who can blot that name
With any just reproach?

CLAUDIO
                    Marry, that can Hero.
Hero itself can blot out Hero's virtue.
What man was he talked with you yesternight
Out at your window betwixt twelve and one?
Now, if you are a maid, answer to this.

HERO
I talked with no man at that hour, my lord.

CLAUDIO
O Hero, what a Hero hadst thou been
If half thy outward graces had been placed
About thy thoughts and counsels of thy heart!
But fare thee well, most foul, most fair! Farewell,
Thou pure impiety and impious purity!

'forehand sin: premarital intercourse. *Large:* immodest. *comely:* decently appropriate.

Seeming: i.e., you only "seem" to be good. *Dian:* Diana, goddess of chastity. *orb:* the moon, Diana's domain. *be blown:* open into bloom.

wide: far from the truth.

60

kindly: natural (i.e., you are both of the same kind).

65

70
Hero itself: the name "Hero."

75

thoughts and counsels: secret thoughts.
80

Claudio exits.

Don Pedro and Benedick assist Hero, now faint with dispair, as she exits.
Leonato remains alone and speaks to the audience.

From the ensemble area, a Male speaks to the audience of his personal distress.

One Woman speaks to another Woman.

The song is sung by a Man first and repeated by a Woman.

Angelo and the Narrator enter the playing area; the Narrator takes the part of Angelo's servant.

For thee I'll lock up all the gates of love,
And on my eyelids shall conjecture hang,
To turn all beauty into thoughts of harm,
And never shall it more be gracious.

for thee: because of your
deceit. *conjecture:* suspicion.

be gracious: seem beautiful.

LEONATO
Hath no man's dagger here a point for me?

85

[*The Passionate Pilgrim*, VII]

MALE
Her lips to mine, how often hath she joined;
Between each kiss, her oaths of true love swearing!
How many tales to please me hath she coined,
Dreading my love, the loss whereof still fearing.
    Yet in the midst of all her pure protestings,
    Her faith, her oaths, her tears, and all were jestings.
She burnt with love, as straw with fire flameth;
She burnt out love, as soon as straw outburneth;
She framed the love, and yet she foiled the framing;
She bade love last, and yet she fell aturning.
    Was this a lover, or a lecher whether?
    Bad in the best, though excellent in neither.
FEMALE
Whom best I love I cross, to make my gift
The more delayed, delighted.
VOICES
Cunning love
Loose love
Unlawful love
Untaught love
Unthrift love
Contemned love
Inflaming love
NARRATOR
Let copulation thrive!

Dreading: i.e., dreading the
loss of.

framed: created (as in building the frame of
something). *foiled:* spoiled.
aturning: turned to other
men. *whether:* which of the
two was she—a lover or a
lecher?

15

Contemned: Despised.

["Take, O, Take Those Lips Away," from *Measure for Measure,* IV.i]

SONG
Take, O, take those lips away
  That so sweetly were forsworn;
And those eyes, the break of day,
  Lights that do mislead the morn.
But my kisses bring again, bring again,
  Seals of love, but sealed in vain, sealed in vain.

25
mislead the morn: trick
morning into believing that
the sun has risen.

12 Bad...neither: the sense is unclear; the line may mean that she was neither a good lover nor a successful lecher.

The Narrator addresses the audience.

The Narrator speaks as a servant.

The servant exits.

Isabella enters, ushered in by the servant. He exits to the periphery.

Isabella starts to leave; Angelo stops her with his words.

Isabella turns to Angelo.

ANGELO

                              Never could the strumpet,
With all her double vigor—art and nature—
Once stir my temper; but this virtuous maid
Subdues me quite. Ever till now,
When men were fond, I smiled and wondered how.

art and nature: false artifice and sensual love. *temper:* temperament (i.e., the mixture of one's humours). *fond:* behaving foolishly in love.

NARRATOR

Here's much to do with hate, but more with love.
Why, then, O brawling love, O loving hate,
O anything, of nothing first create!

35

[*Measure for Measure*, II.iv]

ANGELO

How now! Who's there?

NARRATOR

One Isabel, a Sister, desires access to you.

ANGLEO

Teach her the way. O heavens!
Why does my blood thus muster to my heart,
Making both it unable for itself,
And dispossessing all my other parts
Of necessary fitness?
How now, fair maid?

it: my heart.

ISABELLA

I am come to know your pleasure.

ANGELO

That you might know it would much better please me
Than to demand what 'tis. Your brother cannot live.

it: my pleasure (i.e., desire).

ISABELLA

Even so. Heaven keep your honor!

ANGLEO

Yet may he live awhile; and, it may be,
As long as you or I. Yet he must die.

ISABELLA

Under your sentence?

15

ANGELO

Yea, it is so. Now I shall pose you quickly.
Which had you rather: that the most just law
Now took your brother's life, or, to redeem him,
Give up your body to such sweet uncleanness
As she that he hath stained?

pose you: put a question to you.

20

ISABELLA

                        Sir, believe this:
I had rather give my body than my soul.

Isabella moves closer to him, enthusiastic.

Isabella falls to her knees.

ANGELO
I talk not of your soul. Our compelled sins
Stand more for number than for account.
ISABELLA
                                        How say you?   25
ANGELO
Nay, I'll not warrant that; for I can speak
Against the thing I say. Answer to this:
I, now the voice of the recorded law,
Pronounce a sentence on your brother's life;
Might there not be a charity in sin
To save this brother's life?
ISABELLA
                        Please you to do't,
I'll take it as a peril to my soul;
It is no sin at all, but charity.
ANGELO
Pleased you to do't at peril of your soul
Were equal poise of sin and charity.
ISABELLA
That I do beg his life, if it be sin,
Heaven let me bear it! You granting of my suit,
If that be sin, I'll make it my morn prayer
To have it added to the faults of mine,   40
And nothing of your answer.
ANGLEO
                        Nay, but hear me.
Your sense pursues not mine. Either you are ignorant,
Or seem so craftily, and that's not good.
ISABELLA
Let me be ignorant, and in nothing good,   45
But graciously to know I am no better.
ANGLEO
To be received plain, I'll speak more gross:
Your brother is to die.
ISABELLA
So.
ANGELO
And his offense is so, as it appears,   50
Accountant to the law upon that pain.
ISABELLA
True.
ANGELO
Admit no other way to save his life—

I'll...that: I would not pledge that what I have just said is my true opinion. *for...say:* I can argue the other side just as easily to test you.

Please: If it pleases.

Pleased: If it pleased. *were equal poise:* there would be an exact balance.

nothing of your answer: you would not be answerable for the decision. *Your...mine:* You don't understand me.

graciously: by the grace of God. *received plain:* understood clearly. *gross:* directly, openly.

Accountant: Accountable.

23–24 Our...account: Sins which we are compelled to do are remembered but are not charged against our spiritual account.

The light is now a very tight circle enclosing both Isabella and Angelo within its boundaries.

Angelo circles around Isabella within the area of light.

As I subscribe not that, nor any other,
But in the loss of question—that you, his sister,
Finding yourself desired of such a person
Whose credit with the judge, or own great place,
Could fetch your brother from the manacles
Of the all-binding law; and that there were
No earthly means to save him, but that either
You must lay down the treasures of your body
To this supposed, or else to let him suffer.
What would you do?

ISABELLA
As much for my poor brother as myself:
That is, were I under the terms of death,
The impression of keen whips I'd wear as rubies,
And strip myself to death, as to a bed
That longing have been sick for, ere I'd yield
My body up to shame.

ANGELO
                    Then must your brother die.

ISABELLA
And 'twere the cheaper way.
Better it were a brother died at once
Than that a sister, by redeeming him,
Should die for ever.

ANGELO
Were not you then as cruel as the sentence
That you have slandered so?

ISABELLA
Ignomy in ransom and free pardon
Are of two houses; lawful mercy
Is nothing kin to foul redemption.

ANGELO
                        Let me be bold:
I do arrest your words. Be that you are—
That is, a woman. If you be more, you're none;
If you be one, as you are well expressed
By all external warrants, show it now
By putting on the destined livery.

ISABELLA
I have no tongue but one. Gentle my lord,
Let me entreat you speak the former language.

ANGELO
Plainly conceive: I love you.

ISABELLA
My brother did love Juliet,
And you tell me that he shall die for it.

---

subscribe: agree to.
But…question:
Assuming that nothing
more can be said to defend
Claudio.

60

supposed: fictitious person.
him: Claudio.

terms: sentence.

strip myself: i.e., with the
lash. *That…for:* That
I have longed for.

70

the cheaper way: the better
part of the bargain.

75
slandered so: accused of
cruelty.
Ignomy: Ignominy.
of two houses: very
different. *nothing:* not at
all.
80
arrest your words: hold you
to what you said. *that:* that
which. *If…none:*
You're not a woman if you
try to be more virtuous
than a woman ought to be.
expressed: Displayed. *putting…livery:* behaving as a
submissive woman ought to.

90

Before Isabella can get away, Angelo grabs her and holds her tightly.

Angleo lets Isabella go, and then he leaves her.

The light pinspots Isabella, alone, surrounded by darkness.

Isabella exits.
A man in the ensemble speaks to another man.

ANGELO
He shall not, Isabel, if you give me love.

ISABELLA
I will proclaim thee, Angelo, look for't!
Sign me a present pardon for my brother,

present: immediate.

Or, with an outstretched throat, I'll tell
The world aloud what man thou art.   95

ANGELO
Who will believe thee, Isabel?
My unsoiled name, th'austereness of my life,
My vouch against you, and my place in the State

vouch: sworn testimony.

Will so your accusation overweigh

overweigh: outweigh,
overcome. *in your own*

That you shall stifle in your own report

report: i.e., you will

And smell of calumny. I have begun,

besmirch your own reputa-

And now I give my sensual race the rein.

tion. *my sensual race:* my

Fit thy consent to my sharp appetite;

lustful disposition. *the rein:*

Lay by all nicety and prolixious blushes

free rein. *nicety and*

That banish what they sue for. Redeem thy brother

prolixious: fastidiousness

By yielding up thy body to my will,

and tiresome. *That...*

Or else he must not only die the death,

for: i.e., your behavior

But thy unkindness shall his death draw out

makes me less inclined to

To lingering sufferance. Answer me tomorrow,

be merciful. *unkindness:* un-

Or, by the affection that now guides me most,

naturalness (as a sister

I'll prove a tyrant to him. As for you,

should act to her own

Say what you can; my false o'erweighs your true.

brother). *sufferance:* torture.
affection: passion, lust.

ISABELLA
To whom should I complain? Did I tell this,

Did I: If I were to.

Who would believe me? O perilous mouths,   115
That bear in them one and the self-same tongue,
Either of condemnation or approof,
Bidding the law make curtsy to their will,

make curtsy: give in.

Hooking both right and wrong to th'appetite,
To follow as it draws. I'll to my brother.

as it draws: drags (as an

Though he hath fallen by prompture of the blood,

anchor). *prompture:*

Yet hath he in him such a mind of honor

urging. *mind of honor:*

That, had he twenty heads to tender down

honorable way of behaving.

On twenty bloody blocks, he'd yield them up
Before his sister should her body stoop
To such abhorred pollution.   125
Then, Isabel, live chaste, and brother die;
More than our brother is our chastity.
I'll tell him yet of Angelo's request,
And fit his mind to death for his soul's rest.

MALE
                        I do love her, too;   130
Not out of absolute lust, though peradventure

The Narrator addresses the audience as he surveys his troubled ensemble.

As the Narrator is speaking, Audrey pulls Touchstone into the playing area.

Audrey attempts to push Touchstone to the ground to kiss him.

William enters with a pitchfork over his shoulder. Audrey scrambles to her feet and rearranges her skirt.

William bows politely to Touchstone.

I stand accountant for as great a sin.

NARRATOR

Love is merely a madness, and, I tell you, deserves as well a dark
house and a whip as madmen do; and the reason why they are
not so punished and cured is that the lunacy is so ordinary that the   135
whippers are in love too.

[*As You Like It*, V.i]

TOUCHSTONE

We shall find a time, Audrey. Patience, gentle Audrey. But there
is a youth here in the forest lays claim to you.

AUDREY

Ay, I know who 'tis. He hath no interest in me in the world.   *interest in:* claim to.
Here comes the man you mean.

WILLIAM

Good ev'n, Audrey.   5

AUDREY

God ye good ev'n, William.   *God…ev'n:* God give
                                   you good evening.

WILLIAM

And good ev'n to you, sir.

TOUCHSTONE

Good ev'n, gentle friend. Cover thy head, cover thy head; nay, I
prithee, be covered. How old are you, friend?

WILLIAM

Five and twenty, sir.   10

TOUCHSTONE

A ripe age. Is thy name William?

WILLIAM

William, sir.

TOUCHSTONE

A fair name. Wast born i' th' forest here?

WILLIAM

Ay, sir, I thank God.

TOUCHSTONE

"Thank God"—a good answer. Art rich?   15

WILLIAM

Faith, sir, so so.

TOUCHSTONE

"So so" is good, very good, very excellent good; and yet it is not,
it is but so so. Art thou wise?

WILLIAM

Ay, sir; I have a pretty wit.

TOUCHSTONE

Why, thou sayest well. I do now remember a saying: "The fool   20

Touchstone takes Audrey's hand.

Touchstone takes William's hand.

As Touchstone is about to clasp William and Audrey's hands together, he swipes Audrey away in his own arms. Then he grabs the pitchfork from William's hand and tries to scare him away. William stands firm. As Touchstone runs at William with the pitchfork from all angles, William manages to dodge and evade every attack, effortlessly, while standing in one place.

Touchstone is plainly exhausted, as he sits helpless on the ground. William remains untouched and firm in his place.

William gives into Audrey's plea and finally moves away.
Audrey helps Touchstone up and supports him as they exit. As the three return to the ensemble area, the entire company's earlier angry mood changes, and the members of the ensemble begin to warm to each other. The Narrator senses this shift in disposition and speaks.

Beatrice follows Benedick into the acting area.

doth think he is wise, but the wise man knows himself to be a fool." You love this maid?

WILLIAM
I do, sir.

TOUCHSTONE
Give me your hand. Art thou learned?

WILLIAM
No, sir. 25

TOUCHSTONE
Then learn this of me: To have is to have; for it is a figure in rhetoric that drink, being poured out of a cup into a glass, by filling the one doth empty the other; for all your writers do consent that ipse is he. Now you are not ipse, for I am he.

drink...other: i.e., we cannot both have Audrey. *your writers:* ancient authorities. *ipse:* "he himself" (Latin).

WILLIAM
Which he, sir?

TOUCHSTONE
He, sir, that must marry this woman. Therefore, you clown, abandon (which is in the vulgar "leave") the society (which in the boorish is "company") of this female (which in the common is "woman"); which together is "abandon the society of this female," or, clown, thou perishest; or, to thy better understanding, diest; or, to wit, I kill thee, make thee away, translate thy life into death, thy liberty into bondage. I will deal in poison with thee, or in bastinado, or in steel; I will bandy with thee in faction; I will o'errun thee with policy; I will kill thee a hundred and fifty ways. Therefore, tremble and depart.

clown: rustic, backwoods fellow.

35

bastinado: beating someone with a club. *in steel:* by sword. *bandy with thee in faction:* fight with you as one faction against another. *policy:* cunning.

AUDREY
Do, good William.

WILLIAM
God rest you merry, sir.

NARRATOR
Now does my project gather to a head.
My charms crack not, my spirits obey, and Time
Goes upright with his carriage.

carriage: burden.

[*Much Ado about Nothing*, II.iii]

BEATRICE
Against my will I am sent to bid you come in to dinner.

BENEDICK
Fair Beatrice, I thank you for your pains.

BEATRICE
I took no more pains for those thanks than you take pains to thank me. If it had been painful, I would not have come.

Beatrice, a little stunned by Benedick's changed manner, exits to the ensemble area.

Benedick exits with his newly found love for Beatrice on his mind.

The Narrator addresses the ensemble and the audience. He is giving the cue to the ensemble to patch up their quarrels about love and once again find unity and happiness.

BENEDICK
You take pleasure, then, in the message?   5
BEATRICE
Yea, just so much as you may take upon a knife's point.
BENEDICK
Ha! "Against my will I am sent to bid you come in to dinner." There's
a double meaning in that! "I took no more pains for those thanks
than you took pains to thank me." That's as much as to say,
"Any pains that I take for you is as easy as thanks." If I do not   10
take pity of her, I am a villain; if I do not love her, I am a pagan.
I will go get her picture.
NARRATOR
                                He's fallen in love. Now we
Make peace of enmity, fair love of hate.

The Musician begins to play "A Lover and His Lass"; the Narrator and the other members of the ensemble gather and begin singing, as if they were surrounding a campfire.

As the last chorus is repeated, the ensemble moves out of the acting area in the following pairs: Romeo and Juliet, Portia and Bassanio, Hotspur and Kate, Jessica and Lorenzo, and Beatrice and Benedick. During this exit, the following lines may be heard.
Bassanio talks to Portia.

PART II
Finding Solutions to Love's Problems

NARRATOR
If music be the food of love, play on!

["It Was a Lover and His Lass," from *As You Like It*, V.iii]

SONG
It was a lover and his lass,
   With a hey, and a ho, and a hey nonino,
That o'er the green corn-field did pass
   In the spring time, the only pretty ring time,   *ring time:* time for engage-
When birds do sing, hey ding a ding a ding;   ments and weddings.
   Sweet lovers love the spring.

Between the acres of the rye,
   With a hey, and a ho, and a hey nonino,
These pretty country folks would lie   10
   In spring time, the only pretty ring time,
When birds do sing, hey ding a ding a ding;
   Sweet lovers love the spring.

This carol they began that hour,
   With a hey, and a ho, and a hey nonino,   15
How that a life was but a flower
   In spring time, the only pretty ring time,
When birds do sing, hey ding a ding a ding;
   Sweet lovers love the spring.

And therefore take the present time,   20
   With a hey, and a ho, and a hey nonino,
For love is crowned with the prime   *prime:* spring.
   In spring time, the only pretty ring time,
When birds do sing, hey ding a ding a ding;
   Sweet lovers love the spring.   25

BASSANIO
What made me love thee? Let that persuade thee there's
something extraordinary in thee.

Juliet speaks to Romeo.

Hotspur speaks to Kate.

Cressida speaks to the ensemble.

Lorenzo and Jessica enter the playing area, as soft music plays.

Lorenzo and Jessica sit together surrounded by a magic circle of moonlight.

JULIET
By heaven, I love thee better than myself.
HOTSPUR
Beshrew me, but I love her heartily.
CRESSIDA
I am giddy, expectation whirls me round;   30
The imaginary relish is so sweet
That it enchants my sense.

[*The Merchant of Venice*, V.i]

LORENZO
How sweet the moonlight sleeps upon this bank!   *bank*: hill.
Here will we sit and let the sounds of music
Creep in our ears. Soft stillness and the night
Become the touches of sweet harmony.   *Become the touches:* Are
Sit, Jessica. Look how the floor of heaven   becoming to the notes.
Is thick inlaid with patens of bright gold.   *patens:* thin, metallic plates.
The moon shines bright. In such a night as this,
When the sweet wind did gently kiss the trees
And they did make no noise, in such a night
Troilus methinks mounted the Troyan walls   10
And sighed his soul toward Grecian tents,
Where Cressid lay that night.
JESSICA
                    In such a night,
Did Thisbe fearfully o'ertrip the dew,
And saw the lion's shadow ere himself,   15
And ran dismayed away.
LORENZO
                    In such a night,
Stood Dido with a willow in her hand   *Dido:* queen of Carthage,
Upon the wild sea banks, and waft her love   who was deserted by
To come again to Carthage.   Aeneas. *willow:* symbol of
JESSICA   lost love. *waft:* called back
                    In such a night,   (wafted).
Medea gathered the enchanted herbs
That did renew old Aeson.
LORENZO
                    In such a night,
Did Jessica steal from the wealthy Jew,   25
And with an unthrift love did run from Venice

14 Thisbe: cf. *A Midsummer Night's Dream*, act V.

22 Medea: a witch who helped Jason obtain the Golden Fleece and who enchanted Aeson, Jason's father, so that the old man would be young and handsome again.

They tease each other lovingly.

Lorenzo kisses Jessica.

Hotspur enters the playing area, half-dressed, carrying a letter; upon seeing him, Jessica and Lorenzo exit.

Enter Kate; Hotspur puts on his shirt and begins to pack a duffel bag with his clothing.

Kate begins to help him pack as she speaks.

As far as Belmont.

JESSICA

        In such a night,
Did young Lorenzo swear he loved her well,
Stealing her soul with many vows of faith,   30
And ne'er a true one.

LORENZO

        In such a night,
Did pretty Jessica, like a little shrew,
Slander her love, and he forgave it her.

JESSICA

I would out-night you, did nobody come;   35
But hark, I hear the footing of a man!

footing: footsteps.

[*Henry IV, Part I*, II.iii]

HOTSPUR

"But, for mine own part, my lord, I could be well contented to be there, in respect of the love I bear your house." He could be contented! Why is he not, then? In respect of the love he bears our house! He shows in this he loves his own barn better than he loves our house. Let me see some more. "The purpose you undertake is dangerous." Why, that's certain! 'Tis dangerous to take a cold, to sleep, to drink; but I tell you, my lord fool, out of this nettle, danger, we pluck this flower, safety. "The purpose you undertake is dangerous, the friends you have named uncertain, the time itself unsorted, and your whole plot too light for the counterpoise of so great an opposition." Say you so? Say you so? I say unto you again, you are a shallow, cowardly hind, and you lie! I will set forward tonight. How now, Kate? I must leave you within these two hours.

house: family. *He:* the author of the letter is not identified.

unsorted: inopportune. *for...of:* to counter-balance. *hind:* useless servant.

KATE

O my good lord, why are you thus alone?   15
For what offense have I this fortnight been
A banished woman from my Harry's bed?
Tell me, sweet lord, what is't that takes from thee
Thy stomach, pleasure, and thy golden sleep?
Why dost thou bend thine eyes upon the earth   20
And start so often when thou sit'st alone?
Why hast thou lost the fresh blood in thy cheeks
And given my treasures and my rights of thee
To thick-eyed musing and cursed melancholy?
In thy faint slumbers, I by thee have watched
And heard thee murmur tales of iron wars,

stomach: appetite.

thick-eyed musing: day-dreaming. *faint:* uneasy, restless. *watched:* kept

Kate tries to hold his face in her hands.

Hotspur pulls away from her, stuffing the rest of his clothes in the bag and calling to a servant.

They fight fiercely and lovingly.

Kate hangs on to him.

Hotspur pushes her away.

Speak terms of manage to thy bounding steed,
Cry "Courage! To the field!" And thou hast talked
Of sallies and retires, of trenches, tents,
Of palisadoes, frontiers, parapets,
Of basilisks, of cannon, culverin,
Of prisoners' ransom, and of soldiers slain,
And all the currents of a heady fight.
Thy spirit within thee hath been so at war
And thus hath so bestirred thee in thy sleep,
That beads of sweat have stood upon thy brow
Like bubbles in a late-disturbed stream;
And in thy face, strange motions have appeared,
Such as we see when men restrain their breath
On some great sudden hest. O, what portents are these?
Some heavy business hath my lord in hand,
And I must know it, else he loves me not.

HOTSPUR
What, ho!

KATE
But hear you, my lord!

45

HOTSPUR
What say'st thou, my lady?

KATE
What is it carries you away?

HOTSPUR
Why, my horse, my love, my horse!

KATE
Out, you mad-headed ape!
A weasel hath not such a deal of spleen
As you are tossed with. In faith,
I'll know your business, Harry, that I will.
I fear my brother Mortimer doth stir
About his title, and hath sent for you
To line his enterprise. But if you go...

50

55

HOTSPUR
So far afoot, I shall be weary, love.

KATE
Come, come, you paraquito, answer me
Directly unto this question that I ask.
In faith, I'll break thy little finger, Harry,
An if thou wilt not tell me all things true.

HOTSPUR
Away,
Away, you trifler! Love? I love thee not;
I care not for thee, Kate. This is no world
To play with mammets and to tilt with lips.

60

awake. *manage:* horsemanship.
sallies: attacks. *retires:* retreats. *palisadoes:* stakes set in the ground. *parapets:* low walls or ramparts. *basilisks:* very large cannons. *culverin:* longer, lighter cannons. *currents:* current terms (military jargon). *heady:* headlong, fierce. *motions:* emotions, facial expressions. *hest:* behest, command. *heavy:* important, sorrowful.

spleen: rashness.

title: claim to the throne. *line:* reinforce, support.

paraquito: little parrot.

mammets: dolls.

Kate thinks he is serious, and she moves away from him feeling great sorrow.

Hotspur sweeps Kate up in his arms.

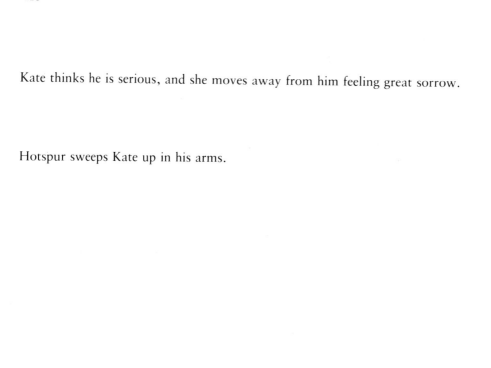

Hotspur turns to leave.

They run together for a last embrace.

As he watches Kate stare at the departing Hotspur, the Narrator speaks the following line. The Narrator addresses the audience.

We must have bloody noses and cracked crowns,
And pass them current too. God's me, my horse! 65
What say'st thou, Kate? What would'st thou have with me?
KATE
Do you not love me? Do you not indeed?
Well, do not then; for since you love me not,
I will not love myself. Do you not love me?
Nay, tell me if you speak in jest or no. 70
HOTSPUR
Come, wilt thou see me ride?
And when I am a-horseback, I will swear
I love thee infinitely. But hark you, Kate:
I must not have you henceforth question me
Whither I go, nor reason whereabout.   *whereabout:* about what.
Whither I must, I must; and, to conclude,
This evening must I leave you, gentle Kate.
I know you are wise, but yet no farther wise
Than Harry Percy's wife; constant you are,
But yet a woman; and for secrecy,   *for:* as for
No lady closer, for I well believe
Thou wilt not utter what thou dost not know.
And so far will I trust thee, gentle Kate.
KATE
How! So far?
HOTSPUR
Not an inch further. But hark you, Kate: 85
Whither I go, thither shall you go too;
Today will I set forth, tomorrow you.
Will this content you, Kate?
KATE
     It must, of force.
NARRATOR
Alas! This parting strikes poor lovers dumb. 90
I talk of dreams,
Which are the children of an idle brain;
Begot of nothing but vain fantasy,   *vain fantasy:* empty
Which is as thin of substance as the air   imagination.
And more inconstant than the wind.   95

---

64 cracked crowns: (1) broken heads and (2) coins with cracks in them; Hotspur plays on both senses of the word "crown." A cracked crown (coin worth five shillings) was worthless as currency, hence the pun in line 65.

Pericles enters and looks longingly at an image in the distance.

Pericles exits to the ensemble area and sits with a female partner.

From the ensemble area, Juliet talks to Romeo, Beatrice to Benedick, Cressida to Troilus, and Hotspur to Kate.

Enter Portia and Bassanio.

[*Pericles*, I.i]

PERICLES
See where she comes, apparelled like the spring,
Graces her subjects, and her thoughts the king
Of every virtue gives renown to men!
Her face the book of praises, where is read
Nothing but curious pleasures, as from thence
Sorrow were ever razed, and testy wrath
Could never be her mild companion.
You gods that made me man, and sway in love,
That have inflamed desire in my breast
To taste the fruit of yon celestial tree
Or die in the adventure, be my helps,
As I am son and servant to your will,
To compass such a boundless happiness!

NARRATOR
And when love speaks, the voice of all the gods,
Make heaven drowsy with the harmony.

JULIET
My bounty is as boundless as the sea,
My love as deep; the more I give to thee,
The more I have, for both are infinite.

BEATRICE
And, Benedick, love on; I will requite thee,
Taming my wild heart to thy loving hand.
If thou dost love, my kindness shall incite thee
To bind our loves up in a holy band.

CRESSIDA
Decline your head. This kiss, if it durst speak,
Would stretch thy spirits up into the air.

HOTSPUR
Excellent wretch! Perdition catch my soul,
But I do love thee! And when I love thee not,
Chaos is come again.

Graces: With graces as.
gives: that gives.
the book of praises: a book containing all possible praiseworthy virtues.
curious: unique, exquisite.
as: as if. *ever razed:* erased forever.
sway: power, rule.
adventure: attempt.

compass: encompass.

15

Taming...hand: a metaphor from hawking.
kindness: i.e., of the same kind.

25

[*The Merchant of Venice*, III.ii]

PORTIA
You see me, Lord Bassanio, where I stand,
Such as I am. Though for myself alone
I would not be ambitious in my wish
To wish myself much better, yet for you

Portia hands Bassanio a ring from her finger.

Bassanio holds the ring with great reverence and love.

The Musician strikes a chord, and the music reflects the loving harmony the couples have reached.

I would be trebled twenty times myself,
A thousand times more fair, ten thousand times
More rich, that only to stand high in your account,
I might in virtues, beauties, livings, friends,
Exceed account. But the full sum of me
Is sum of something, which, to term in gross,
Is an unlessoned girl, unschooled, unpracticed;
Happy in this, she is not yet so old
But she may learn; happier than this,
She is not bred so dull but she can learn;
Happiest of all is that her gentle spirit
Commits itself to yours to be directed,
As from her lord, her governor, her king.
Myself and what is mine to you and yours
Is now converted. But now I was the lord
Of this fair mansion, master of my servants,
Queen o'er myself; and even now, but now,
This house, these servants, and this same myself
Are yours, my lord's. I give them with this ring,
Which when you part from, lose, or give away,
Let it presage the ruin of your love,
And be my vantage to exclaim on you.

BASSANIO
Madam, you have bereft me of all words.
Only my blood speaks to you in my veins,
And there is such confusion in my powers
As, after some oration fairly spoke
By a beloved prince, there doth appear
Among the buzzing pleased multitude,
Where every something, being blent together,
Turns to a wild of nothing, save of joy
Expressed and not expressed. But when this ring
Parts from this finger, then parts life from hence.
O, then be bold to say Bassanio's dead.

NARRATOR
How's the day?

MALE
On the sixth hour, at which time, my lord,
You said our work should cease.

NARRATOR
                            I did say so.

VOICES
Love wrought these miracles
My love is a fever
I love thee, and it is my love that speaks
I love thee more and more

---

account: opinion, estimation. *livings:* possessions. *account:* estimation.
Is sum of something: I have some small worth. *to term in gross:* to state fully.
Happy: Fortunate.

15

from: if by.

But now: Till now.
20

ruin: decay.
vantage: opportunity. *exclaim on:* accuse.

powers: faculties.
30

wild: wild amount.
35

be bold to say: announce with full confidence.
How's the day: What time of the day is it?

40

45

The music stops. The lights fade on the lovers kissing; the Narrator looks at the couples and the audience.

Dearest chuck
By heaven, I love thee better than myself.
NARRATOR
My lord and lady, it is now our time,
That have stood by and seen our wishes prosper,
To cry, good joy! Good joy, my lord and lady!   50
VOICES
Best love
Ever-lasting love
Unstrained love
Dearest chuck
Fair love   55
Pretty sweeting
Good love
Ah, sweet ducks
Inflaming love
NARRATOR
This rough magic I here abjure.   60
BENEDICK
Love, and be silent.

End of Act Two

COMMENTARY
MUSIC
LIST OF SCENES
SUGGESTED READING

Commentary

For page numbers to individual scenes, please see "List of Scenes."

Act I, part I of *Shakespeare's Lovers,* "Discovering Love," begins with a litany of terms of endearment taken from a variety of Shakespearean sources. The Narrator introduces the play to the audience, and a gay Renaissance dance leads into act I, scene v from *Romeo and Juliet.*

In this scene, Romeo and Juliet meet for the first time at a formal ball given by the Capulets, Juliet's family. Since Romeo is from a rival family, the Montagues, his presence at the ball places him in serious danger. By isolating the two lovers early in his play, Shakespeare allows his audience to focus on the manner in which adolescent infatuation grows to love of tragic stature. The dialogue between Romeo and Juliet, which takes the form of a regular English sonnet (three quatrains and a couplet), plays on the idea of pilgrimage and adoration of Saints as a metaphor for the devotion of love. Readers familiar with the play may recall that Romeo has recently expressed his eternal love for another young woman, Rosaline, in the previous scene, hence his sudden declaration of love for Juliet may be suspect. As Romeo begs first one kiss, then another from Juliet, her innocent distrust of flowery speech and behavior becomes evident. "You kiss by the book" may be Juliet's way of upbraiding Romeo for spending too much time learning the rituals of love and not enough practicing sincerity. Or, the line may become a true compliment, depending upon how the director wishes to interpret it.

The next scene, taken from *The Tempest* (III.i), features Miranda, daughter to the magician Prospero, and Ferdinand, son of Alonso, king of Naples. Twelve years ago, Prospero was deposed as Duke of Milan by his brother, Antonio, and Alonso, and set adrift with his infant daughter. Reaching an enchanted island, the two have made a home for themselves surrounded by spirits and monsters. On this day, a storm brings the ship of Antonio, Alonso, and Ferdinand near the island, and Prospero causes the three to be washed ashore by the power of his magic. Ferdinand and Miranda meet and instantly fall in love. So that his beautiful, young daughter will not be won too easily, Prospero commands the boy to carry heavy logs as a test of his sincerity. One of Shakespeare's most forthright and charming creations, Miranda has seen no other men during her lifetime than her father and Caliban, a deformed son of the witch Sycorax. Her love for Ferdinand is firm and sincere; "I have no" ambition / To see a goodlier man," she tells her father after first meeting the young prince. Ferdinand, too, is spontaneously drawn to Miranda's freshness, her unadorned beauty, and her simple honesty. Their union is an optimistic conclusion to Prospero's desire for revenge on the usurpers of his throne and betokens a move toward order and harmony in society, which have been generated out of the love, magic, and art of Prospero's island.

The following delightful scene from *The Taming of the Shrew* (III.i) introduces three characters from the subplot of that play: Lucentio (in love with Bianca, disguised as a Latin scholar to be near her), Hortensio (also in love with Bianca, disguised as a teacher of music), and Bianca herself (daughter to Baptista and sister to the shrewish Kate). Both men are courting the lady, and both are attempting to woo her while they pretend to be her teachers. Shakespeare elicits great comic value in this scene, as he does in the entire play, by toying with the various levels of "poses" and "supposes" adopted by the characters. Lucentio, for example, must reveal himself and his declaration of true love to the coy Bianca without allowing Hortensio, who is already suspiciously jealous, to discover his proper identity. Hortensio, who calls himself "Litio," pledges his love to the lady as he sings (quite awkwardly, we assume) the musical scale; Lucentio, who eventually wins Bianca, makes love to her as he translates Ovidian Latin. Feigning interest in all her suitors, Bianca enjoys sporting with their affections. In a play filled with mistaken identities, role reversals, and other farcical confusions, this episode is a typical example of Shakespeare's early genius as a writer of dramatic comedy.

After a brief narrative bridge, we move to a more sordid love affair from *Troilus and Cressida* (III.ii). Set within a leering, satirical play about the excesses of the Trojan War, the love between Troilus and Cressida seems doomed before its beginning. Brought together by Pandarus, Cressida's overzealous uncle, the lovers swear eternal devotion on one day, and Cressida proves unfaithful on the next. The fervor of the love between Miranda and Ferdinand has soured in this new atmosphere of disease, lost honor, lethargy, and lust.

The rank promiscuity of *Troilus and Cressida* is scant preparation, however, for the macabre, violent view of love presented in the next scene from *Richard III* (I.ii), in which one of Shakespeare's most Machiavellian villains attempts to seduce a woman whose husband and father-in-law he has recently murdered. Richard is not so much deformed physically as he is deformed mentally—a monster of a man whose perverted ambition makes him grasp for the throne regardless of its moral cost. Richard's wooing of Anne, motivated by a desire to strengthen his claim to the throne of England, is a triumph of the power of words over a woman whose ethical resolve has been weakened by grief. Throughout the scene, Richard appeals to Anne's vanity by arguing that his great love for her has caused him to kill her relatives. The shifting moods of the scene are apparent and instructive. Anne begins in bitter anger and ends in confused submission; Richard, on the other hand, initiates his attack with flattery, mock sincerity, and humility, and concludes with a chilling, boastful soliloquy. All passions exhibited in the scene are heightened beyond normal limits. Most spectators of the play share Anne's confused appraisal of Richard's character. We shudder at his blatantly sardonic behavior, yet most of us also admit to a fascination with his obvious power over the course of human destiny.

The play's mood is lightened immediately by the lilting "Who Is Silvia" (*Two Gentlemen of Verona*, IV.ii), a Petrarchan song in praise of feminine beauty, which introduces two successive scenes from *Henry V.*

The first of these, taken from III.iv, centers upon Katherine, daughter to the king and queen of France, and her lady-in-waiting, Alice, as the princess attempts to learn as much English as possible before the visit of King Henry. The mood of the scene is rushed, somewhat playful, and ironically condescending as Katherine memorizes a language that she no doubt considers crude and barbaric. Comic mispronunciations throughout culminate in the confusion of the English words "foot" and "count" with two French obscenities. The scene's laughter dissolves into a rather formal confrontation between the princess and the English king.

More comfortable as a soldier than as a lover, Henry is obliged to court Katherine for political expediency; he needs to solidify his claim over French territory won recently in battle. In this scene (V.ii), Shakespeare's ideal Christian king shows that his awkwardness on the battlefield of love is charmingly effective due to its blend of honesty, straightforwardness, broken French, and true affection for the likeable young Princess. "Nice customs curtsy to great kings," argues Henry, and the kiss he wins from Kate symbolizes the union of two cultures and two important European nations.

Despite the happy conclusion of this romantic interlude, part I of *Shakespeare's Lovers* ends in confusion prompted by the earlier scenes from *Troilus and Cressida* and *Richard III* and by the natural loss of enthusiasm following the ecstasy of love. The Narrator introduces the second part of the first act, "Seeking Advice about Love," which displays characters who need help in dealing with newly acquired feelings of self-doubt and fear about love.

Speed and Launce, two farcical servants from *Two Gentlemen of Verona* (III.i), offer a comic parody of the motif of true friendship and ideal love in the main plot of that play. Launce's catalogue of the various vices and virtues of his unnamed mistress is a vaudevillian treatment of the love-seriousness we have encountered earlier with Romeo and Juliet, Miranda and Ferdinand, and Bianca and Lucentio. Laced with obscene puns and gestures, this scene reminds us abruptly that love in the lower classes can be coarse, mundane, matter-of-fact, and outrageously funny—however secret and troubled it may be.

The next scene, also from *Two Gentlemen* (I.ii), has two ladies of nobility fighting over a different piece of paper. Julia, while bantering with her maid, Lucetta, tries to hide the fact that she loves Proteus, a handsome young man who will shortly be sent to Milan by his father. Given a letter sent by her lover, Julia feigns indifference, then tears the note to shreds before the bemused Lucetta (so that the maid will not suspect her love for Proteus). After the maid's departure, Julia frantically tries to piece the letter back together so that she can read it. Julia's faithfulness to the fickle Proteus is apparent here, and it foreshadows her ultimate forgiveness of the manner in which Proteus betrays both his lover and his friend.

An immediate contrast to Julia's steadfastness in love is provided by the behavior of Benedick in the next scene from *Much Ado about Nothing* (I.i). A perpetual bachelor and self-styled woman hater, Benedick scorns the infatuation of his friend Claudio for a mild, modest young woman named "Hero." As we learn later in the play, Benedick is himself in love with Hero's cousin Beatrice, a sprightly feminist who is able to match Benedick blow-by-blow in their loving battle of the sexes. In this scene, Benedick's wry cynicism is a comic prelude to his ludicrous lovesickness later in the play. By giving us two views of the nature of love, Shakespeare teaches that the conventional Petrarchan relationship between Claudio and Hero is doomed to problems, while the seemingly less stable union between Beatrice and Benedick will thrive because it is based upon honesty, mutual respect, imagination, and immense energy.

In the forest of Arden, Rosalind and Orlando are in love (*As You Like It*, III.iv). Disguised as a boy for her safety (and to test the strength of Orlando's affection), Rosalind asks Orlando to court her as if she were his true love, instead of the young man she appears to be. In this scene, Rosalind and Celia, a friend, bemoan the fact that Orlando has not met them in the forest as he had promised. Celia delights in teasing the normally sensible Rosalind about her love-sick behavior. Beneath this exterior of disguise and feminine commiseration lies an important theme: Rosalind, who is emotionally more mature than Orlando, must teach the young man the ways of love before he is truly worthy of her devotion. In the regenerative "green world" of the forest, the harmonizing power of their love helps to restore order in the rest of the play's comic environment.

Brief scenes from *Romeo and Juliet* (I.i) and *As You Like It* (II.iv) are followed by a profusion of unhappy, dejected, complaining lines about the unkindness of love. The Narrator is unable to calm the ensemble's mood of unrest, and the first act ends on this note of confusion.

Act II, part I, "Having Problems with Love," begins with Benedick's rather misogynistic soliloquy from II.iii of *Much Ado about Nothing*, which is followed immediately by a demonstration of his cynical attitude toward women in a confrontation with the witty Beatrice (I.i). Both Beatrice and Benedick feign hostility to protect themselves from the pain of unrequited love. The ensemble still disturbed as they were at the conclusion of act I, divide into male and female "camps" on the stage and speak bitter lines about the unfaithfullness of love.

Phebe, in the next scene from *As You Like It* (III.v), represents this scornful nature of love as she rejects the attentions of Silvius, a shepherd who dotes on her incessantly. The two embody such Petrarchan stereotypes that Rosalind, still disguised as a boy, enters and begins to instruct Phebe and Silvius on the proper behavior of amorous young shepherds. The plan backfires, however, when Phebe falls in love with Rosalind in her guise as Ganymede. Later, Rosalind admonishes Silvius for doting on Phebe—an unworthy object of his love. Offering a comic parody to the main plot's theme of the education of lovers, this scene juxtaposes rural and courtly attitudes toward the virtues necessary in a steadfast relationship. As he does in many of his other comedies, Shakespeare deliberately contrasts different views of the nature of love—here with at least a hint of homosexuality in Phebe's attraction to a girl disguised as a boy.

The comic caricature of love presented in *As You Like It* shifts abruptly to angry accusations about faithlessness and fallen morals in the next scene from *Much Ado about Nothing* (IV.i). Falsely slandered by a plot laid by the unscrupulous Don John, Hero is accused of infidelity by Claudio. In this scene, Hero is entirely surrounded by men, and she becomes the victim in a world dominated by male suspicions about the deceptive ways of women. Claudio's superficial demeanor and his too-conventional expectations of love have been shattered easily by Don John's ruse, as have the shocked protestations of Hero been overcome by the clamor of male egos.

Stanza VII of *The Passionate Pilgrim* echoes this same theme of feminine unfaithfulness and bridges the gap between Hero's betrayal and an even more sinister plot of infidelity in love from one of Shakespeare's darkest comedies, *Measure for Measure* (II.iv). In this scene, Angelo, the newly appointed Duke of Vienna, forces a cruel choice upon Isabella, a young woman about to become a nun. Knowing that her brother, Claudio, has been imprisoned and sentenced to death for the crime of "fornication" (impregnating his beloved, Juliet, prior to their marriage), Isabella appears before Angelo to beg for her brother's life. Seized with lust for the woman and sensing the power of his new office, Angleo offers to free Claudio if Isabella will make love with him. Prizing her honor and fearing everlasting death, Isabella refuses: "Better it were a brother died at once / Than that a sister, by redeeming him, / Should die forever," she reasons. Set within its sordid context of sexual desire and abuse of authority, Isabella's chaste reply is a spiritual response in a world too given to moral depravity. One of the play's chief horrors lies in the ease with which Angelo allows his love for Isabella to distort his "outward-sainted" demeanor; warped by lust, his highly intelligent, penetratingly introspective mind turns criminal in pursuit of Isabella's virtue. These characters are two of the most fascinating ever created by Shakespeare.

A touch of comedy from *As You Like It* (V.i) replaces the gloom of seduction with the bright laughter of rural courtship. Touchstone, a royal jester transplanted to the forest of Arden, is in love with Audrey, a country wench. In this scene, Touchstone stakes his amorous claim on Audrey by vanquishing William, a dull country bumpkin. Much of the scene's humor lies in the contrast between the polished wit of the professional fool and the innocent stupidity of his rural antagonist. Touchstone attempts to overwhelm William with the force of words, while William seems wonderfully oblivious to the jester's verbal and intellectual superiority.

The Narrator's intent to reconcile all the lovers of the ensemble seems close to being realized, especially in light of the brief, humorous scene which follows from *Much Ado* (II.iii) in which Benedick's love-foolishness toward Beatrice begins to show.

Part II of the second act, "Finding Solutions to Love's Problems," begins with a rousing song from *As You Like It* (V.iii), continues with a series of short speeches from one lover to another, and finally settles into a scene from *The Merchant of Venice* (V.i) in which Lorenzo and Jessica, two lovers, trade mythic stories describing the firmness of their commitment to each other. After references to Troilus and Cressida, Pyramus and Thisbe, Dido and Aeneas, and Medea and Jason, Lorenzo and Jessica elevate their own love to the level of mythology:

> In such a night,
> Did Jessica steal from the wealthy Jew,
> And with an unthrift love did run from Venice
> As far as Belmont.
> In such a night,
> Did young Lorenzo swear he loved her well,
> Stealing her soul with many vows of faith,
> And ne'er a true one.

The entrance of Hotspur shifts the scene to II.iii of *Henry IV, Part I*. A rebel lord, Hotspur has apparently sent out letters inviting other English lords to join him in overthrowing the king, Henry IV. The letter he is reading at the outset of the scene, written by a lord who declines to participate in the rebellion, so angers the rash Hotspur that he tears it to shreds on stage. The questions which follow from his spirited, loving wife, Kate, imply clearly that she knows exactly why he is preparing for battle (to take the throne on behalf of his brother-in-law, Mortimer). Shakespeare deliberately gives us several such glimpses of Hotspur's private, domestic life in an attempt to humanize the character and to emblemize the clash of feudal factions by the personal conflict between Hotspur and Prince Hal (later to become Henry V). The love between Kate and Hotspur is so strong, so mature that we cannot help feeling some sympathy and admiration for this man who plans to usurp the English throne and who dies in the attempt.

After a brief speech from *Pericles* (I.i) in which the title character praises the beautiful daughter of Antiochus, king of Antioch, several pairs of lovers introduce the conclusion of the casket scene from *The Merchant of Venice* (III.ii). Bassanio, suitor to the wealthy, wise, and lovely Portia, has won her for his wife by choosing the proper casket (in a test stipulated by Portia's father's will). In this section of the scene, the proper choice has been made, and Portia, rejoicing at her good fortune, describes the terms of her dowry. This last union of lovers, this bringing together of man and woman, symbolizes the marriages of all the other true couples in *Shakespeare's Lovers*: Romeo and Juliet, Ferdinand and Miranda, Lucentio and Bianca, Troilus and Cressida, Julia and Proteus, Henry and Katherine, Beatrice and Benedick, Rosalind and Orlando, Touchstone and Audrey, Hotspur and Kate, and Lorenzo and Jessica. With a final litany of love, the play ends as it began: The lovers kiss, the lights fade, and the Narrator concludes his magic.

MUSIC

Who is Silvia?[1]

[1]Since the Shakespearean music for this song is no longer extant,
the authors have included Schubert's famous version.

she;___ The heaven such grace did lend___her,

That she_ might_ ad- mir- ed___ be,___

That she might ad- mir- ed_ be.

A Song to the Lute in Music

(When Griping Griefs)
by Richard Edwards

When grip- ing griefs___ the heart doth wound,

And dole- ful dumps the mind_____ op- press,

Then mu- sic with_____ her sil- ver sound

With speed- y help doth lend re- dress.

Take, O, Take Those Lips Away
by John Wilson

Take,_____ O, take those lips _____ a- way That so

sweet- ly were for- sworn; And those eyes, the__ break of day,

Lights that do mis- lead the__ morn. But my kiss- es

bring a- gain, Seals of __ love, but sealed in vain.

It Was a Lover and His Lass

Anon.

It was a lov- er and his lass, With a hey, and a ho, and a hey non- i- no, And a hey, _____ non- i- no, no, no.

That o'er the green corn- field did pass In spring time, in spring time, in spring time, the on- ly pret- ty ring time, When

birds do sing, hey ding a ding a ding, hey ding a ding a ding, hey

ding a ding a ding. Sweet lov- ers love the spring.

List of Scenes

ACT I

ACT II

Suggested Reading

Renaissance Life and Society

Allen, Don Cameron. *The Star Crossed Renaissance*. Durham, N.C.: Duke University Press, 1941.

Berlin, Normand. *The Base String: The Underworld in Elizabethan Drama*. Rutherford, N.J.: Fairleigh Dickinson University Press, 1968.

Bradford, Gamaliel. *Elizabethan Women*. Edited by Hardol Ogden White. Boston: Houghton Mifflin, 1936.

Camden, Charles Carrol. *The Elizabethan Woman*. Houston: Elsevier Press, 1952.

DuBoulay, F.R. *An Age of Ambition: English Society in the Late Middle Ages*. London: Nelson Press, 1970.

Dusinberre, Juliet. *Shakespeare and the Nature of Women*. New York: Barnes and Noble, 1975.

Eagleton, Terence. *Shakespeare and Society*. New York: Schocken, 1967.

Harrison, G.B. *England in Shakespeare's Day*. London: Methuen, 1928.

Horne, Herman. *Shakespeare's Philosophy of Love*. Brandenton Beach, Fla: Horne, 1946.

Kott, Jan. *Shakespeare Our Contemporary*. New York: Doubleday, 1964.

LeChapelain, Andre. *The Art of Courtly Love.* New York: F. Ungar, 1941.

Murstein, Bernard I. *Love, Sex, and Marriage Through the Ages.* New York: Springer Publishing Company, 1974.

Nelson, John Charles. *The Renaissance Theory of Love.* New York: Columbia University Press, 1955.

Partridge, Eric. *Shakespeare's Bawdy.* London: Routledge and Kegan Paul, 1955.

Pearson, L.E. *Elizabethan Love Conventions.* New York: Barnes and Noble, 1967.

Scaglione, Aldo P. *Nature and Love in the Late Middle Ages.* Berkeley: University of California Press, 1963.

Sullierot, Evelyne. *Women on Love: Eight Centuries of Feminine Writing.* New York: Doubleday, 1979.

Uyuyan, John. *Shakespeare and the Rose of Love: A Study of Early Plays in Relation to the Medieval Philosophy of Love.* New York: Barnes and Noble, 1960.

————*Shakespeare and Platonic Beauty.* New York: Barnes and Noble, 1961.

Wilson, John Dover. *Life in Shakespeare's England.* Cambridge: Cambridge University Press, 1926.

Actors and Acting

Bradbrook, Muriel C. *The Rise of the Common Player: A Study of Actor and Society in Shakespeare's England.* London: Chatto and Windus, 1962.

Brown, Ivor. *Shakespeare and the Actors.* London: Bodley Head, 1970.

Brown, John Russell. *Shakespeare's Plays in Performance.* London: Methuen, 1966.

Harbage, Alfred. *Shakespeare's Audience.* New York: Columbia University Press, 1941.

Joseph, Bertram. *Elizabethan Acting.* Oxford: Oxford University Press, 1951.

Speaight, Robert. *Shakespeare on the Stage: An Illustrated History of Shakespearean Performance.* New York: Little, Brown, 1973.

Sprague, Arthur Colby. *Shakespearean Players and Performances.* Cambridge, Mass.: Harvard University Press, 1953.

Styan, J. L. *Shakespeare's Stagecraft*. Cambridge: Cambridge University Press, 1967.

The Comedies

Barber, C. L. *Shakespeare's Festive Comedy*. Princeton: Princeton University Press, 1959.

Champion, Larry S. *The Evolution of Shakespeare's Comedies*. Cambridge, Mass.: Harvard University Press, 1970.

Charlton, H. B. *Shakespearean Comedy*. London: Methuen, 1938.

Felperin, Howard. *Shakespearean Romance*. Princeton: Princeton University Press, 1972.

Frye, Northrop. *A Natural Prespective: The Development of Shakespearean Comedy and Romance*. New York: Columbia University Press, 1965.

Hunter, Robert G. *Shakespeare and the Comedy of Forgiveness*. New York: Columbia University Press, 1965.

Lawrence, W. W. *Shakespeare's Problem Comedies*. New York: F. Ungar, 1960.

Leggatt, Alexander. *Citizen Comedy in the Age of Shakespeare*. Toronto: University of Toronto Press, 1973.

———*Shakespeare's Comedies of Love*. London: Methuen, 1974.

McFarland, Thomas. *Shakespeare's Pastoral Comedy*. Chapel Hill: University of North Carolina Press, 1972.

Palmer, John. *Comic Characters of Shakespeare*. London: Macmillan, 1946.

Phialas, Peter G. *Shakespeare's Romantic Comedies: The Development of Their Form and Meaning*. Chapel Hill: University of North Carolina Press, 1966.

Richmond, Hugh M. *Shakespeare's Sexual Comedy*. Indianapolis: Irvington Press, 1971.

Stevenson, David Lloyd. *The Love-Game Comedy*. New York: Columbia University Press, 1946.

Tillyard, E. M. W. *Shakespeare's Early Comedies*. New York: Barnes and Noble, 1965.

Traversi, Derek. *Shakespeare: The Early Comedies*. London: Longmans Green, 1960.

The Tragedies

Brodwin, Leonora L. *Elizabethan Love Tragedy, 1586-1625.*
New York: New York University Press, 1971

Campbell, Lily Bess. *Shakespeare's Tragic Heroes: Slaves of
Passion.* Cambridge: Cambridge University Press, 1930.

Dickey, Franklin M. *Not Wisely But Too Well: Shakespeare's
Love Tragedies.* San Marino, Calif.: Huntington Library
Press, 1957.

Mason, Harold A. *Shakespeare's Tragedies of Love.* London:
Chatto and Windus, 1970.

Stilling, Roger. *Love and Death in Renaissance Tragedy.*
Baton Rouge: Louisiana State University Press, 1976.